WITH TIME TO SPARE

The Ultimate Guide to Peak Performance for Entrepreneurs, Adults with ADHD and other Creative Geniuses

Linda Walker

CREATIVE GENIUS PUBLICATIONS
MONTREAL

Publisher: Creative Genius Publications, Montreal, Quebec Canada

ISBN 978-0-9869556-0-0

Cover design and interior book design/layout by SpicaBookDesign
www.spicabookdesign.com / (250) 661-7512.

Dedicated to
Duane Gordon, my dear husband
Jennifer and Kyrie Anne Gordon, my beloved daughters
Your courage, love, and generosity are such an inspiration to me.

ACKNOWLEDGEMENTS

+ I am so grateful to *Duane Gordon*, my husband, my soul mate and my best friend, a man who is also an artist, entrepreneur and poster child for ADHD. He inspired me to write this book, and I will be forever grateful for his encouragement, patience, insights and unconditional love. I thank him also for his editing skills.

+ I want to thank my daughters, *Jennifer* and *Kyrie*, for allowing me to see this truly wonderful and amazing world through their eyes, a second chance to see it for the first time. I'd like to honor my mom, *Micheline*, and my father, *James*, for their unconditional love and support.

+ I'd like to acknowledge *Kimberly Hains* for helping me make this project a reality. A million thanks to *Laila Beaudoin* for your friendship, wisdom and for lighting the way.

+ Special thanks go to *Ava Green* and *Andrea Wilde* for taking time to read my manuscript and providing your helpful feedback. Your input molded this book — and its author — into shape.

+ I would like to pay tribute to my clients for allowing me the privilege of witnessing their greatness and for inspiring me with their resilience and courage.

+ And finally, I am forever grateful to God for the gifts she has bestowed upon me.

TABLE OF CONTENTS

PREFACE xi

INTRODUCTION xv

PART 1. BUILD A FIRM FOUNDATION 1

Chapter 1.   Does Productivity Kill Creativity? 5
Chapter 2.   Creative Geniuses Think Differently.... 9
Chapter 3.   Building Blocks for Success................. 23

PART 2. REALIZE YOUR DREAMS 43

Chapter 4.   Set SMARTer Goals 45
Chapter 5.   Get Motivated, Stay Motivated........... 57
Chapter 6.   Practice Layered Learning 69
Chapter 7.   Achieve with Action 77
Chapter 8.   Create the Simplest Possible System 81
Chapter 9.   Hone Your Habits 91

PART 3. BUILD ON YOUR NATURAL
RHYTHMS.. 103

Chapter 10. Tap Into Your Natural Rhythms.......... 105
Chapter 11. Map Your Tasks 117
Chapter 12. Perform at Your Peak 123

PART 4. WEAPONS OF MASSIVE
            PRODUCTION 127

Chapter 13. Set Effective Boundaries 131
Chapter 14. Declutter Your Life 137
Chapter 15. Break Bad Habits Before
             They Break You 149
Chapter 16   Eradicate Time Traps.......................... 157
Chapter 17. Stop Doing the Wrong Thing 161

PART 5. TAKE CHARGE 169

Chapter 18. Select the Proper Tools...................... 173
Chapter 19. Plan For Success................................ 195

PART 6. PAVE THE WAY FOR CHANGE.......... 209

Chapter 20. Conquer Procrastination Now.............. 211
Chapter 21. Managing Expectations 253

PART 7.   FINAL OUTCOMES 259

           AFTERWORD 265
           INDEX.. 267
           RESOURCE GUIDE 283
           ABOUT THE AUTHOR........................ 285

PREFACE

W*ith Time to Spare* is a labor of love. The story of how this book came to be is filled with hardship, struggle and misery. But it's also a story of compassion, hope and success. Living with ADHD, whether you have it yourself or are living with someone struggling with it, can be challenging. More than that, it can be frustrating, maddening and incomprehensible. On the other hand, it can also be exciting, endearing and funny.

With Time to Spare shares lessons learned in the "School of Hard Knocks." My husband, Duane, has ADHD. He received his diagnosis following my youngest daughter, Kyrie's diagnosis when she was six years old. Our first decade of marriage was about survival, and as a new wife and mother, instability and insecurity were constant companions, companions I could have done without.

Duane couldn't keep a job, let alone choose a career. Impulsive and forgetful, Duane wasn't much help around the house either. Never lazy, Duane worked long hours, quickly rising through the ranks at company after company until he lost interest and either quit or was "advised" to seek new opportunities elsewhere. Suspecting that if he couldn't work for someone else, he was destined to own his own business, we also pursued several entrepreneurial ventures with similar results. We were always at the brink, the brink of financial ruin and the brink of divorce.

Many people wonder how Duane feels when I share the struggles early in our marriage. Duane has read every word I've written and approved each passage. In fact, he often insists, "Don't sugar coat it. We have to share the unvarnished truth." His fear is that people struggling with ADHD will conclude that, "Sure, it's fine for him. His life wasn't that bad, but MY life is really screwed up! Nothing can help me!" As he says, "This approach works, and we have to get that message through to people." And he's right. The strategies revealed in *With Time to Spare* work, and if you or someone you love is struggling with ADHD, I wrote this for you.

There is no magic pill or "one size fits all" solution, but these effective strategies were developed over several years with Duane and I working together. Guided by Duane's ADHD coach, we were able to discover previously unknown strengths and talents that enabled Duane to not only hold a job but to truly excel in his career. He was also able to become the husband and father he'd always wanted to be, vastly improving his relationships with his daughters and me. You'll learn more throughout *With Time to Spare,* but suffice it to say, the "diamond in the rough" I'd married became a real gem.

For many years, I didn't know what I wanted to be "when I grew up." I knew I wanted to make a positive difference, and I wanted to do it in a way that has a big impact on people's lives. With the changes Duane was making in his life (and our lives), I was no longer just focused on survival. Drifting through life seizing opportunities as they appeared had resulted in a successful corporate career but I was left uninspired. I didn't feel I was pursuing my true calling, and I certainly wasn't having the positive impact on people's lives I craved.

When I considered careers that have a positive impact, I couldn't help but think of Duane's ADHD Coach. Her work with Duane certainly made a positive difference in his life. And by helping him, she improved my life and the lives of our children, and positively affected the lives of our family, friends and Duane's colleagues at work. The ripple effect is incredible and continues to this day. Teaching people to deal effectively with ADHD, to enable them to tap into their potential rather than succumbing to the symptoms and the struggle, has the far-reaching impact I'd been looking for.

Each of us has something unique and valuable to contribute. You have amazing skills and talents, and when you work with your strengths and pursue your passions, you can change the world, your world, and the worlds of the people around you. If you've felt resigned, destined never to reach your full potential because every ounce of energy is taken up simply surviving, I'm asking you to try at least one more time. Success doesn't go to those who never fail, it belongs to those who never surrender.

In *With Time to Spare*, I've shared stories of people just like you, people who were struggling. They never surrendered and by applying the same strategies we'll explore together, today they are free to pursue their passions. Their stories inspired me to write this book, and I hope you'll be as inspired as I was, and that you'll come to believe life can be more than you imagined. Like you, each of them they had a life that was "draining the life out of them," and by removing the obstacles and taking a stand for who they are, be it entrepreneur, artist, adult with ADHD or other Creative Genius, they were able to really live their life and make the huge contribution that is theirs alone to bring to the world.

TO RECEIVE YOUR FREE GIFT RESERVED ESPECIALLY FOR YOU,
AS A READER OF WITH TIME TO SPARE.

WWW.COACHLINDAWALKER.COM/WITHTIMETOSPARE

INTRODUCTION

Are you busy? I don't mean busy, but collapse-at-the-end-of-the-day-drained-and-drag-yourself-out-of-bed-too-soon-the-next-morning-still-exhausted busy? Are you running in place, never seeming to make any headway? Do you wonder despairingly if this is all there is? Are you frustrated because your great ideas never come to fruition? Do you feel that you spend most of your time forcing yourself to do things in which you have no real interest interspersed with only infrequent moments when you are free to express your real potential?

Many of the counter-intuitive strategies we share will improve anyone's productivity under the right conditions. And unfortunately, economic woes, ever increasing demands for profit and increased global competition are creating these conditions ever more frequently. Overloaded schedules and unrealistic expectations often lead to an inability to focus, impulsiveness, disorganization, procrastination and overwhelm, symptoms eerily similar to those of Attention Deficit Hyperactivity Disorder; it is not surprising ADHD-friendly productivity-improving strategies can help.

When I worked in the corporate world, I managed an impossibly under-staffed project. I worked 16-hour days all week and an extra 8 to 10 hours every weekend trying to keep up, but had I known and applied these strategies at the time, I would have led a much more balanced life. The project was exciting but important things such as family, friendships, my health and my personal projects took a back seat.

There are people, however, who don't fit the standard mold. Their brains actually work differently than most, making them better suited to creativity than conformity, a difference that appears as an inability to focus, impulsiveness and disorganization when they're forced to be conventional. These people are also frustrated that they can't find time and energy to express their creativity because they're overwhelmed by a long list of to-dos and the chaos of their lives.

Many of them have tried various time management systems and productivity tricks handed down to them by their parents and friends, but none of it works for long. Out-of-the-box approaches can sometimes solve conventional problems, but it's rare that a traditional approach can resolve an unconventional problem. Now they're resigned to a life that's out of control, facing high levels of stress and burnout or worse, hopelessness. As a result they are never free to make the true contribution that burns inside them and their families, friends, colleagues and communities miss out.

Whether you're an entrepreneur, an artist, a professional who relies heavily on your creativity or an adult with ADHD, you are more than likely one of these people; you're a Creative Genius. And if you're a Creative Genius struggling to survive, hoping to thrive in a crazy-busy world that doesn't work the way you do, this book is for you.

Creative Geniuses are a constant source of new ideas. Your brain works differently than most, making connections others miss, each connection a new idea and the seed for a chain of new thoughts and concepts. Controlled, this cognitive hyperactivity presents a unique advantage in a world that values ideas, but unchecked, the flow of ideas can be so distracting you have difficulty functioning in your daily life. In extreme cases, these same symptoms diagnose as Attention Deficit Hyperactive Disorder (ADHD).

As a Creative Genius, you're a non-conformist, solving problems intuitively rather than methodically, spotting out-of-the-box solutions others overlook, and you are capable of achieving more, *much more!* At least you suspect you will be if, 1) you can turn your brilliant ideas into successful endeavors, 2) you can get and stay organized and, 3) you can finish your many projects.

Dozens of ideas pop into your head, each more amazing than the last. This constant flow of creative brilliance distracts you, because as you chase each new idea, you're unable to stick with any one long enough to develop it fully and reap the benefits. In the end, all you have to show for your genius is dozens of unfinished projects and an untouched To-Do list.

Of course, having your fingers in so many pies results in a constant flow of emails, phone calls and interruptions that also make it difficult for you to focus on one thing at a time. Overwhelmed by your many tasks, projects and fires to put out, you can't decide where to start. You change strategies and plans often, procrastinate on boring but essential tasks and as a result, miss many opportunities. Guilt often drives you to tackle just one more thing – after all, it will only take 10 minutes (in reality it takes 30) – so you're often rushed and late for appointments and stuck in the office long after you promised you'd be finished.

You arrive home at the end of a very long day, exhausted. You've expended all your energy and so have nothing left to give to your family, to your friends and worse, to yourself. You'd like to have a hobby or to take on a project just for fun, but you brush your own needs aside, feeling unfulfilled. Each New Year, you resolve that this year will be different, but for many Creative Geniuses, January 1st marks another year of regrets and unrealized potential.

Time management courses, books on work-life balance and advice from friends and family provide no relief. Linear approaches to time management treat hours in your day like inventory on a shelf, but you can't "manage" time. You can't stockpile it, speed it up, slow it down or buy more should you run out. You're a Creative Genius and you need strategies to improve your productivity, but these strategies must work *with* your unique brain instead of against it. Trying to "control" your brain is no more effective than trying to cork a volcano!

With Time to Spare is based on strategies developed in *The Maximum Productivity Makeover for Creative Geniuses*, a coaching program developed by and for Creative Geniuses, which uses an approach that takes advantage of your natural abilities, putting *you* at the center of your life, not some inventory of hours. Working with your brain's natural abilities instead of against them allows you to achieve more without leaving you depleted. Using these strategies, you'll manage your life by taking advantage of peak performance strategies, easily eliminate obstacles and be on your way to reaching your most ambitious goals.

You have already taken an enormous step in the right direction, a step most people never take. Rather than surrendering, resigning yourself to average – or worse – you've taken action. The average person never reads another book after leaving high school. You're obviously above average, but even more, as a Creative Genius struggling to succeed in a world where conformity is the norm, saddled with traditional tools that don't work the way you do, to have accomplished what you have already represents an enormous victory.

I believe you are destined for greatness. In fact, I believe the solutions to most of the world's problems will come from the minds of Creative Geniuses. I don't know exactly what your contribution will be, perhaps you don't know yet either, but I do know that you have in your hands the strategies that will enable you to overcome obstacles that have been slowing your progress your entire life. The results you desire are here for the taking, now it's up to you to pursue your passions. Continue reading, but don't just read; I challenge you to implement the strategies revealed in *With Time to Spare*. Experiment, discover what works for you, and apply those strategies to create the life of your dreams.

PART ONE
BUILD A FIRM FOUNDATION

CHAPTER 1
Does Productivity Kill Creativity?

CHAPTER 2
Creative Geniuses Think Differently

CHAPTER 3
Building Blocks of Success

PART ONE. BUILD A FIRM FOUNDATION

I know you're eager to get started but before you can truly embrace strategies like the ones described in this book, you must be ready to accept and adopt new ways of doing things. Creative Geniuses often have a love-hate relationship with productivity. You want to get more done because it would make your life easier, because people want you to do more and because you feel overwhelmed and imagine that if you could "just get through this (and this and this and this!)" it would solve all your problems.

But I've seen many people who swear they're committed to reaching their objectives fail to even get out of the starting gate because they haven't taken time to set in place a solid foundation for what's to come. That's because while you know everyone, yourself included, wants you to get more done, inside you suspect they have no idea just how hard you work already, and that maybe, just maybe, the solution is for everyone to GET OFF YOUR BACK!

If you're open to considering a new approach to productivity, and you've been completely unaffected by people's insistence that you should "stop making excuses," "try harder" and "live up to your potential," congratulations on coming through unscathed! On the other hand, if you might feel any lingering guilt or resentment that could make you resist new ideas or different approaches, especially those that go against "the way things are supposed to work," the lessons of the next three chapters will be particularly valuable. (And if you're sure you're ready, humor me and work through Part I anyway.)

Part I is your opportunity to explore your relationship to productivity. As a Creative Genius, you've realized that traditional ways of doing things don't work for you, but you may have also been led to believe that this is your fault, that indeed, there is something wrong with you. If we don't deal with these beliefs, we risk attempting to build a bright new future on a foundation of shifting sand. Working through Part I will create a solid foundation by shifting and aligning your beliefs so that as you transform your life, you do so with confidence that you are honoring the real you.

CHAPTER ONE

DOES PRODUCTIVITY KILL CREATIVITY?

Creative Geniuses often resist strategies to improve their productivity because they feel productivity and creativity are mortal enemies. Nothing could be further from the truth. In this chapter, we challenge some myths about productivity, particularly as it relates to creativity and consider a more holistic view of productivity in your life.

Most of us equate productivity with performance at work. You may even resist becoming more productive. After all, you're already too busy! And productivity has become a scary word; employers always want to increase productivity to increase profits, often laying off co-workers and ask you to do more with less! "Doing more" when you're already doing too much is unfair. No wonder you might be put off by the thought of increasing your productivity.

However, I take a holistic view of productivity seeing it as the way you apply all your energy to all the elements of your life. Productivity incorporates all tasks, projects and activities that support you, allow you to progress toward your personal goals and keep you healthy and stress-free.

PRODUCTIVITY IS HOW YOU APPLY YOUR ENERGY TO ALL THE ELEMENTS OF YOUR LIFE.

Many people address business demands for more output by working longer hours, working through lunch and foregoing exercise or relaxation to buy more time. They compound this error as, stressed and worried about their jobs, they lose sleep and make the situation worse.

A holistic or whole-person approach to productivity will help you be more effective in your life. You can have the life you want, including time for your family and friends, involvement in your community and the pursuit of personal goals. This approach will make you more efficient so you can get everything in your life done with minimum effort. You'll work and live in a better-organized, more competent way and maintain control over every aspect of your life.

> YOU CAN HAVE THE LIFE YOU WANT, INCLUDING TIME
> FOR YOUR FAMILY AND FRIENDS, INVOLVEMENT IN YOUR
> COMMUNITY AND THE PURSUIT OF PERSONAL GOALS.

You won't deplete your energy reserves trying to keep up with the demands in one area (work, for example), so you'll have energy remaining to reach your full potential as a whole person. You'll have time and energy for family and friends, for exercise, to sleep and to eat nutritiously, for taking care of financial and health-related commitments and you'll have time for yourself, time to pursue your own personal objectives.

People often believe stress results from having too much to do. They advocate doing less to reduce stress, but living demands a certain amount of effort. You need time and energy to work so you can meet your financial needs, exercise, get enough sleep, feed yourself appropriately, pay your bills, do your taxes, take care of your family and maintain and develop enriching relationships.

Studies show it's not the things you have accomplished that cause your stress. It's the things you have not completed that weigh most heavily on your mind. Worry about how and if you can accomplish these things cause the most stress. Most of us have so many distractions we become disorganized, leaving us even less productive. Physical and mental disorganization affects Creative Geniuses more than most because your brains constantly generate your own added distractions in a churn of ideas.

In *With Time to Spare*, you'll learn strategies to become better organized. As you improve your productivity, the balance will shift. As you get things done, you'll have fewer things left to weigh on your mind, and you'll have energy left to accomplish the things you find most satisfying.

Many Creative Geniuses consider it impossible to be organized and productive. You worry that imposing structure on your life will somehow limit your creativity. However, I've witnessed it firsthand, so I know you can be productive and have work-life balance without giving up any of the wonderful things that make you "you". In the coming chapters we'll show you how.

CONCLUSION

You can now see that productivity is not simply about "doing more." A holistic view of productivity makes you more effective in the activities that support you, be they financial, professional or career activities, supporting your family and building relationships or maintaining your health, and leave you more time and energy to pursue personal goals and passions.

CHAPTER TWO
||||||||||||||||||||||||||||||

CREATIVE GENIUSES THINK DIFFERENTLY

Guys may not face this problem, but ladies, I'm sure you can relate. Though we come in all shapes and sizes, every time I buy pantyhose, I encounter the "one size fits all" myth. I often see people edging nervously away from me as I mutter under my breath, "One size doesn't fit me!" In this chapter, we'll challenge the premise that "one size fits all." It's not true for pantyhose, and it's not true for time management or personal productivity strategies.

Traditional approaches to improve productivity do not mesh with the way the Creative Genius brain works. We'll also explore what it is that makes you so different, not to make excuses but as a foundation to enable you to choose strategies that take advantage of your unique brain wiring. In this chapter, we'll also get to meet the Creative Geniuses I mentioned earlier, the ones who will serve as our case studies who will "demonstrate" the strategies by implementing them in their lives.

I'm always astounded when time management and productivity improvement programs promise to help everyone. Many of these programs are excellent and meet the needs of many people, particularly "neurotypicals." "Neurotypical" is the term we'll use to describe people who tend to be more linear than a Creative Genius. They complete task Number 1 before they do task Number 2. They prefer a methodical approach, with more planning than spontaneity. Of course, the world couldn't get along very well without "neurotypicals," but you can see why a Creative

Genius might struggle with a time management system created for these people.

Time management systems are not "one size fits all," and if you've ever tried a traditional approach to time management, you've likely discovered that one size doesn't fit you! While you may think you and your Creative Genius brain are the problem, you are not at fault. Even well meaning people (parents, teachers, employers, etc.) who tried to teach you how to be more productive didn't realize that strategies they use might not work for you. They didn't realize that your creative mind works differently.

||||||||||||||||||||||||||||||||||||||||||||||||||||||||||||||||||||||||||||||||||||||||||||||||||||||||||||||||||

TIME MANAGEMENT SYSTEMS ARE NOT "ONE SIZE FITS ALL".

||||||||||||||||||||||||||||||||||||||||||||||||||||||||||||||||||||||||||||||||||||||||||||||||||||||||||||||||||

With Time to Spare is based on *The Maximum Productivity Makeover for Creative Geniuses* coaching program developed to help Creative Geniuses succeed in the world without losing your spark, that magic you bring to everything you touch. Many of the things you learn may seem counter-intuitive but this is only your past programming interfering with what you "feel" is true. In fact, if you "go with your gut", your Creative Genius, rather than your logical brain, you will find this approach very intuitive. This doesn't mean it will necessarily be easy to implement. After all, you will have to undo years of programming and then reprogram your self-management style to reflect your very special qualities.

INTEREST RATHER THAN IMPORTANCE ACTIVATES YOUR BRAIN

Creative Geniuses are interest-based performers. Of course, some people insist everyone is an interest-based performer, but there is an important difference. "Neurotypicals," when faced with boring but essential or important tasks are able to activate their brains enough to focus and complete those tasks, in other words, buckle down and get it done.

CREATIVE GENIUSES ARE INTEREST-BASED PERFORMERS.

Creative Geniuses, faced with similar boring but important tasks, despite recognizing their importance and having a genuine desire to complete them, struggle to maintain their focus. Your creative, imaginative brain finds it difficult, even impossible to stay fully engaged.

Interest activates your brain. There are benefits to being an interest-based performer. As a Creative Genius you are usually interested in subjects and activities where you excel because you love the feeling of being "in the zone" and you want to return to it often. The more you practice your talents, the better you become. When you're in the zone, there are no obstacles, everything is easy and your thoughts flow. My clients tell me it feels amazing; it feels so good, they often find themselves in "hyperfocus". Hyperfocus happens when you focus on one thing to the exclusion of everything else. Creative Geniuses slip into hyperfocus far more easily than most.

Because you want to re-engage in interesting and strength-based activities, you practice them often enough to achieve excellence. Your greatest potential lies in working with and developing your talents and strengths. If everyone, Creative Geniuses and neurotypicals were to develop their talents and strengths instead of struggling to improve their weaknesses to reach, at best, mediocrity, humankind would have already solved many of the problems that plague the world. This is a bold statement, but imagine everyone on Earth doing what they are good at, strong in and passionate about. There would be no stopping us.

YOUR GREATEST POTENTIAL LIES IN WORKING WITH AND DEVELOPING YOUR TALENTS AND STRENGTHS.

Unfortunately, you must also attend to tasks you don't enjoy and that require you delve in your weaknesses. The good news is that *With Time to Spare* will provide solutions for managing those tasks too.

CREATIVE GENIUSES ARE BIG-PICTURE THINKERS

Visionaries, Creative Geniuses are rarely obsessed with details and tend to see the "Big Picture." You have a vision of your objective before you figure out how to achieve it. Visionary thinking makes you a great candidate for entrepreneurial endeavors, as long as you work with neurotypicals to attend to the details.

This big picture thinking increases your chances for success when you start with your vision for your life, choosing your business or career as a vehicle to fulfill your vision. You must clearly define your vision so you feel what it will be like once you achieve your objective. We'll discuss this more in detail in Chapter 3.

CREATIVE GENIUSES ARE PRONE TO INTUITIVE LEAPS AND CONNECTIONS

Creative Geniuses are prone to intuitive leaps, making connections others miss. You suddenly have a brilliant idea for solving a problem or for a new product or service. You're so excited; you immediately start to implement it. You're working away, even making significant progress, until you have another brilliant idea. This new idea is even more brilliant than the first. Ooops! Then it happens again: you have another even more exceptional idea, and off you go. By the end of the day, you've chased several ideas and thoughts, you've even started to work on several projects but you haven't actually completed anything. Unfortunately, your intuitive leaps rarely provide you the satisfaction of seeing your ideas come to fruition.

Staying focused on one idea long enough to fully develop it is a challenge for you. You often find yourself chasing ideas down rabbit holes. Having a vision for your life can help you focus on making decisions as to which idea warrants the greatest effort. Each time an idea pops in your head, ask yourself, "Will this idea move me toward my vision and my goals or will it distract me from them?"

If you feel it will move you toward your vision and goals, then consider your current focus. Does this new idea improve on your current focus or detract from it? If it detracts but it's still a great idea you'd like to develop, write it in a notebook or Idea Journal for future reference. When your current project is finished, you can always go back to your Idea Journal.

CREATIVE GENIUSES GET EXCITED BY NOVELTY AND PASSION

Have you ever found yourself saying YES or volunteering for a project just because you found it so exciting? Maybe it was the project owner's enthusiasm, or that thinking about the project had you generating one brilliant idea after another, but whatever it was, you've now made a commitment you can't possibly meet without other aspects of your life suffering the consequences. In addition, you volunteered without a clear idea of the scope of the project or knowing what they expect from you.

Many Creative Geniuses find themselves overwhelmed. You don't know what to tackle next because your already overstuffed To-Do List can't take another project (most Creative Geniuses don't use an agenda properly or at all). To make things worse, it's too late to back out. That's why one of the first things you'll learn is how to develop the habit of taking time to consider the implications before you commit. We'll address this in more detail later.

CREATIVE GENIUSES ARE ADRENALINE JUNKIES

You can easily spend hours watching television, surfing the Web or playing video games. All these sources of high stimulation help your brain focus. However, these activities do nothing to move you toward your goals. In fact, they keep you from realizing your dreams by creating distractions that are difficult to resist.

SOURCES OF HIGH STIMULATION HELP YOUR BRAIN FOCUS.

Additionally, your addiction to television or computers may prevent you being creative. You use them to relax but these activities don't recharge your energy. Some scientific studies reveal that the longer you watch television, the more difficult it becomes for your brain to recharge.

Video or online games can also be addictive. Some Creative Geniuses indulge their need for adrenaline by participating in extreme sports or other risky activities. Others use a safer but more self-destructive outlet: waiting until the last minute to tackle any task, counting on the rush of a looming deadline to overcome their lack of interest. Unfortunately, this approach results in work that's not up to your true potential. It also often aggravates your co-workers, partners or other people counting on you.

With Time to Spare will teach you to harness your amazing talent and create your own adrenaline by doing those things that give you the most pleasure. You'll learn how John, Sonia, and Patrick, three Creative Geniuses, overcame past programming and moved forward using their natural talents and qualities to create a life that not only allowed them to be more productive at work but improved their work-life balance and personal development.

LET ME INTRODUCE OUR CASE STUDIES

I based two of our cases, John and Patrick, on actual clients who completed *The Maximum Productivity Makeover for Creative Geniuses* program. The last case, Sonia is a composite of several entrepreneurial clients who share many of the same issues. I chose to create a composite as most of my entrepreneurial clients come to me at different stages of their business and after having resolved some issues on their own. My entrepreneurial clients usually have had to deal with the same issues. Creating Sonia from these common issues allows you see the issues common to entrepreneurs and the progress required to manage it. You could say that in Sonia live Ann, Anna, John, Andrew, JP, Veronica, MJ, Clem and many more. Introducing and tracking the participation of all of these players would have made it impossible to see the process required for an entrepreneur to create a powerful and successful life. I've changed all names to maintain privacy, because they are not important here and because I keep all clients' names confidential. These cases will help you see how the strategies of *The Maximum Productivity Makeover for Creative Geniuses* can apply to your own life. Enjoy the journey!

SONIA, THE SERIAL ENTREPRENEUR

Meet Sonia, a serial entrepreneur. She comes to me because she has been struggling with work-life balance. Her first business was a retail store with which she had great early success but soon she grew bored with it. Many of her good clients reduced their purchases dramatically as a cost-cutting measure to help survive the recession. Several didn't survive. As a result, bad debts became a normal occurrence, and after several years struggling to make ends meet, she finally decided to close that business.

Five years ago, she started a construction company. For a couple of years she worked with her small crew; then referrals from satisfied clients soon made her business very popular. Her secret was her ability to anticipate potential issues with designs clients wanted. She was able to explain these design flaws successfully and to offer better alternatives. Clients appreciated this and as a result, she quickly became popular. Getting into this industry was difficult for her and she is somewhat of a pioneer. She really enjoys what she does and the value she offers her clients. She's especially proud as a woman succeeding in a non-traditional industry.

Married with two children, she struggles to maintain a sane work-life balance. Her husband works full-time and takes university classes. She handles most of the household and child-rearing duties. While she worries about her children, she also bears the responsibility of ensuring her two work crews stay employed. She must continue to drum up more business and ensure suppliers are paid. She works an average of 14 hours a day and spends weekends catching up on paperwork, so her only "break" from work is when she helps her learning-disabled youngest daughter with homework.

She has amazing marketing ideas for her business, more than she can ever execute in her lifetime, and she feels she lacks focus. She's pulled in every direction and feels overwhelmed.

She spends her time in sales, prospecting, preparing proposals, invoicing, payroll, sales taxes forms and other government paperwork. She struggles with prospecting and to complete her paperwork, which has led to a few periods where she had no work for her crews. Paperwork is always a problem: final invoicing happens weeks after project completion so cash flow issues are a normal occurrence.

She has also lost contracts because she's late completing and submitting proposals, and she's paid fines because she's late filing her income and sales tax reports. She's overwhelmed with daily decisions, from purchasing paperclips, to buying and fixing the coffeemaker to ordering supplies.

To help her achieve Work-Life Balance, we set objectives for improving her productivity, streamlining her business processes to allow her to delegate more, particularly tasks she hates to do and tends to procrastinate on. We also include long-term growth and exit strategies. Many entrepreneurs, especially serial entrepreneurs, grow bored with their businesses in the absence of start-up challenges and need either an exit strategy or a growth strategy to overcome their loss of interest as the business matures.

PATRICK, THE ARTISTIC SOUL

Meet Patrick: Patrick comes to coaching in search of a "normal" life. His first objective is to keep his job, which is in jeopardy. He's always felt he does not live up to his true potential.

He was so ineffective at work that he has been demoted. His boss gave him three months to improve his productivity or he'd be out of a job. His family is one paycheck away from bankruptcy because he's also an impulsive buyer; he spends without thinking of the consequences.

Married with two young daughters, their financial situation is precarious. In the not too distant past, the family had the phone and cable cut for non-payment. They've had a lien put on his house and Patrick's wages were garnished. Currently, their credit cards are maxed out and bill collectors call because he forgets to mail the checks; his wife has taken over managing the household finances. Patrick and his wife fight over money, argue about the distribution of chores and worry about his precarious work situation. They are under a lot of stress. Patrick also battles obesity, has not seen a doctor or dentist in years and doesn't exercise.

Further discussion reveals that Patrick is a talented artist but never attended art school or pursued his dreams because of his father's objections. He no longer practices his art because he doesn't have time to devote to it. Despite his wife's encouragement and the joy he gets delighting his young daughters with drawings he does for them, he feels conflicted about becoming an artist. He enjoys his work but often finds himself at the office late because of his poor time management. When he finally does come home, he has no energy to do anything. His wife also works full time.

Patrick feels he's not pulling his weight at home, relying on his wife to take care of things more than he'd like to admit. He'd like to help with household chores but doesn't seem to be able to execute them. His wife does most of the household chores, deals with the budget, helps the kids with homework and many other things Patrick can't handle. At the end of the day, they are both so tired they do nothing but sit around and watch TV.

Our first task is to improve Patrick's vision for his life. Having a "normal" life is not very compelling. He is also determined to work on controlling his agenda and keeping his commitments at work and at home. He sets objectives to improve his health and to develop a richer relationship with his wife whom he considers his soul mate.

JOHN, STRUGGLING WITH ADULT ADHD

Now, meet John, a project manager in a high-tech company. He is involved with several sports teams whose schedules can be quite difficult to juggle given the number of projects he tends to work on at the same time. He comes to me to improve his productivity at work. He and his wife are getting a divorce and he wants to be a better role model for his sons.

John works in a cubicle, which creates some distractions. John recently discovered he has Attention Deficit Disorder, also known as Attention Deficit Hyperactivity Disorder (ADD or ADHD), following his son's diagnosis. The cubicle offers no privacy or noise dampening, so when someone talks on the phone or to colleagues, he finds it distracting. With no door, his colleagues tend to drop in and interrupt him. John is amazingly focused in a crisis and so he's become the "go-to" guy to resolve the numerous crises that seem to permeate the company he works for. Unable to concentrate, he jumps from one project to another, never accomplishing much.

He also participates in several meetings each day. Known as a very creative person, his colleagues often invite him to brainstorming meetings. While he appreciates the recognition for his ideas and he enjoys being the hero, it does eat up his time.

To make up for lost time, he wakes up at 5 am and checks emails during breakfast. He takes the train to work so he can get started on work. He rarely eats lunch, but at the end of the day, he's never done his work, so he stays late to complete last-minute deliverables. He only leaves the office when his growling stomach disturbs him at 10 pm and he notices for the first time that everyone has left the building.

Knowing he is always behind, he buys time to complete his assignments by giving himself as much as a month's leeway for his deliverables to his team. Despite the long lead-time, he still waits until the last minute. He once worked 36 hours straight to deliver a project on time. He routinely does the same with his paperwork and, of course, his expense reports are always late.

John wants to become more effective at work. We set a target for him to be able to finish work at 5 pm most evenings so he could be more involved in his sons' lives.

We'll be working through *The Maximum Productivity Makeover for Creative Geniuses* with Sonia, Patrick and John. If you're reading this book because you face similar issues, you'll certainly relate to one or more of our Creative Geniuses. I'll share how we resolved their challenges and I'll offer other solutions our three friends may not have used but that have resolved issues common to Creative Geniuses with other clients.

CONCLUSION

By dispelling the myth that one approach to productivity improvement will or even should work for everyone, hopefully you're now more aware of your own unique qualities. As a Creative Genius, your brain activates with interest, novelty, passion and high stimulation. These characteristics enable you to invest enormous amounts of energy in things that are truly important, interesting and exciting for you. For someone in search of a rewarding life, this is a very positive trait. However, uncontrolled, this tendency can prevent you from achieving your goals as your attention wanders from one stimulating activity to another, or focuses only on highly stimulating but addictive activities.

We've seen how Creative Geniuses are "big picture" thinkers who are often able to make connections others miss, a quality that allows you to be creative, out-of-the-box thinkers. In school or other areas where conformity is valued, this quality can be troublesome, but in the right situation, it can provide real advantages. The Maximum Productivity Makeover for Creative Geniuses was created with these attributes in mind and so focuses on providing the strategies that allow you to take advantage of your unique qualities.

We also met our case studies:

+ Sonia is a serial entrepreneur struggling to keep her life balanced between building her business and supporting her family at home. She feels her inefficiency keeps her working longer hours and while she values her creativity, she worries that her constant flood of innovative ideas is distracting her from taking full advantage of existing opportunities.

+ Patrick is an artist who feels stuck in a corporate life that saps all his energy and keeps him from contributing at home and pursuing his true passion, his art.

+ John is an adult struggling with ADHD who spends most

of his time putting our fires at work. He has developed a bad habit of procrastinating and using the adrenaline created by the fear of looming deadlines to finish his work. However, rushing from deadline to deadline has created an environment where he has no time to prevent crises but spends long hours rushing from one emergency to the next.

- ✦ Creative Geniuses are interest-based performers

- ✦ Your greatest potential is in developing your talents, strengths and interests

- ✦ Creative Geniuses are big-picture thinkers

- ✦ Creative Geniuses are prone to intuitive leaps and make connections others miss

- ✦ Creative Geniuses often don't stay focused long enough on one idea to develop it fully

- ✦ Creative Geniuses are excited by novelty and passion

- ✦ Creative Geniuses tend to use adrenaline to stimulate their brain

CHAPTER THREE

||||||||||||||||||||||||||||||||||||

BUILDING BLOCKS FOR SUCCESS

We want, even expect, instant gratification. We must be able to solve any problem immediately, ideally by taking a pill, but certainly with no effort on our part. Modern society also teaches us "doing" and "having" is more important than "being." However, you can do very little and still have a huge impact on the world. Or you can work very hard, doing more every day, while ultimately accomplishing little and creating little value for the world. It all depends on what you're doing; are you doing the right things or the wrong things?

If you're tempted to skip this section and jump ahead to learn the things you can "do" to improve your productivity, such as how to manage your time, how to overcome procrastination, and so on, please bear with me. In fact, the more you want to jump ahead, the more carefully you need to read this section because it will have a huge impact on your future success. In this section, we examine three factors that determine the effectiveness of all your effort. Now things start getting exciting!

In this chapter, we'll see how to overcome your resistance to change (we all resist change) by creating a compelling dream and feeding it. You'll begin to identify your limiting beliefs, learn to question them and discover how to replace them with more empowering beliefs. And finally, you'll learn that to reach your full potential, you'll need to spend far more of your time and energy developing your talents and strengths than you do on compensating for your weaknesses, while at the same time you honor your values and ensure you have everything in place to meet your own needs.

THE DREAM PUTS THE TIGER IN YOUR TANK

Achieving any goal demands change. We all resist change, and we usually rely on willpower to overcome that resistance. But willpower wears out fast… usually long before the necessary change is complete or permanent.

WILLPOWER WEARS OUT FAST… USUALLY LONG BEFORE THE NECESSARY CHANGE IS COMPLETE OR PERMANENT.

Years ago, an oil company, Esso, marketed their gasoline using a tiger as a mascot, suggesting that putting their fuel in your car was like putting "a tiger in your tank." Just as your car needs fuel to get you where you want to go, you need fuel to reach your objectives too. Your dreams provide the tiger in your tank. Picture your dream clearly in your mind, so clearly you can already feel as if you achieved your goal. How will your life improve when you have a better relationship with your spouse? Will you look forward to coming home at the end of the day? Will you feel anticipation preparing for your next date? Will you relax on the weekend instead of worrying about your spouse's mood? Why do you want to be in control of your life? Do you want to free up your time to pursue a hobby, or do you want a promotion so you can afford to buy a cottage in the country?

Whatever your dream, always keep it active in your mind. Find or create ways of visualizing it, hearing it, experiencing it. Picture yourself in the dream, get a photo of the dream, or even better, get a photo of you experiencing the dream! If you dream of having more time to enjoy a hobby, take a short workshop so you have a chance to experience it. If you're saving for a down payment on a cottage, visit open houses, ask a friend if you could borrow their cottage for a night or rent a cottage for a weekend and "live the dream"; see how it feels.

If you want more success out of life than seems possible now:

1. Picture your dream so clearly you can feel it and find ways to keep it alive,
2. Establish forward-moving goals so you're advancing toward your objective instead of running away,
3. Define it clearly so you'll know when you've achieved it!

Your dream gives you energy to keep going. Later, we'll see how you can keep your dream alive and use it when your resolve flags. Don't set your sights too low. Aim higher than a "normal" life. Normal is not compelling enough. You think you want to be normal but deep down inside, you suspect you're destined for more. You set your sights on a normal life because right now even that seems impossible to achieve, but you're a Creative Genius. Once you learn to harness the power of your creative mind, you'll leapfrog right past normal and on to greatness. Most people dream of doing extraordinary things and of leaving a legacy. You opt for "normal" when you think it's all you can have. But you can have so much more.

AIM HIGHER THAN A "NORMAL" LIFE. NORMAL IS NOT COMPELLING ENOUGH.

When you aim too low, when things get difficult, and they will if you want to change, you don't have a compelling reason to continue. Change is difficult. It requires that you move out of your comfort zone. Humans take the path of least resistance. That made sense for our ancestors who had to survive very difficult conditions. When it's a struggle just to find food or shelter, achieving great feats is not usually on your mind. Patrick is a good example. His financial situation is precarious; his job is hanging on by a thread; his marriage is shaky; his health is very bad. So he aims for survival, aka "normal."

> " TWO ROADS DIVERGED IN A WOOD, AND I – I TOOK THE ONE LESS TRAVELED BY, AND THAT HAS MADE ALL THE DIFFERENCE.
> ROBERT FROST

However, even to get to "normal," Patrick must change the way he does things and resist the temptation of his old ways; that will be tough and a dream of being "normal" is just not going to provide the necessary motivation. His situation is temporary.

Challenging goals provide energy and power when you're facing difficulty. Of course, you must want it. You must want it so bad you can taste it so that in turn, it will energize you and fuel your passion. A dream like that gives you hope when all seems bleak.

Your dreams allow you to feel what it will be like when you achieve your goals. Emotions stick in your memory more than facts. The feelings your dream provokes give you the conviction to make it happen. Get in touch with what you really, really, really want in your life. Ask yourself, if you believed your dream would definitely come true (even if you don't right now), what would you dare dream?

THE EMOTIONS YOUR DREAM PROVOKES GIVE YOU THE CONVICTION TO MAKE IT HAPPEN.

Once you know what it is, your next step is to develop a way to keep it in front of you.

Sonia, like many entrepreneurs, has several big dreams. She wants to become a role model for women succeeding in a man's world against all odds. She also dreams of teaching and helping others to succeed by selling her business concept as a franchise. She'd also like to travel with her husband at least once a year.

After helping Patrick understand why he needs a big dream, he set his sights on becoming a creative leader in the company he works for. He also wants to continue a loving relationship with his wife. Of course, he doesn't develop this ability to dream big all at once. Later, you'll see how his dream develops over time.

John's big dream is to one day be a good role model for his sons. He and his wife are beyond reconciling as she refuses to believe his ADHD diagnosis is anything but an excuse. However, he knows it explains his need to do things differently, and what's more, as ADHD is hereditary, both his sons have it too, and they face the same challenges he does. He wants his sons to feel unconditional love and acceptance and to achieve success in whatever they want to do despite ADHD. It's important to him that he set the example for his sons as someone doing just that. He wants to become someone they can trust to keep commitments. He missed much of their lives working late. He wants more time to spend having fun with his boys. He dreams of owning a cottage in the woods where he and his sons can go on weekends and in the summer to fish and swim.

With a dream like that, how can John fail? He'll let nothing stop him as he refuses to let his children down.

Take some time to construct your life vision. Imagine you've already achieved the vision and answer the following questions. Write the answers down as if you had already achieved your vision.

✦ What does your vision look like? Describe it as if you were living it right now.

✦ Where do you live?

✦ Whom do you share your life with?

✦ What qualities do you possess? Who have you become in the process of achieving this vision?

YOUR BELIEFS MOVE YOU FORWARD OR HOLD YOU BACK

Your beliefs, especially those you hold about yourself, either move you forward or hold you back. If you think you are capable of amazing success, it's likely that orienting your life to fit this belief will lead to success. When faced with challenges, you'll be more likely to look for solutions since you believe you can overcome any challenge. If your belief in yourself is very low, your unthinking reaction when faced with challenges is to retreat like a wounded animal. You form strong beliefs about yourself when you keep your commitments to yourself.

YOUR BELIEFS, ESPECIALLY THOSE YOU HOLD ABOUT YOURSELF, EITHER MOVE YOU FORWARD OR HOLD YOU BACK.

Self-esteem grows by following through on small commitments. If you can honor your commitments, especially to yourself, you'll have a great foundation for feeling good about yourself.

SELF-ESTEEM GROWS BY FOLLOWING THROUGH ON SMALL COMMITMENTS.

A lifetime of being told NO, being called stupid, lazy, a dreamer or worse influence your belief in your abilities - this is the message John had heard all his life. He is very intelligent, but he struggled to pay attention to what was going on around him, often lost in his thoughts, intrigued by new ideas that would pop into his mind. His mountain of unfinished projects fueled his parents, and later his wife, to believe he was lazy.

BE AWARE OF YOUR BELIEFS

My clients often ask me, how does anyone overcome a lifetime of negative feelings? To overcome these beliefs, first become conscious of the limiting beliefs you have about yourself. Look for their source. What led you to hold the beliefs you do?

For a long time, Patrick did not pursue his passion for art because to be a "real artist", he'd have to be a starving artist. Deeply committed to his family, he doesn't indulge his fantasy that he could be an artist, for it would put them at a disadvantage financially. When we look for the source of this belief, Patrick realizes it stems from a situation with his father. Patrick had won a scholarship at a prestigious art school but his father had refused to let him go because he insisted Patrick could never make enough money to support a family from his art. You can ask the same questions Patrick uses to determine the beliefs that hold you back:

- ✦ What beliefs don't serve you anymore?
- ✦ What's the real source of the belief?
- ✦ What's the cost of holding this belief?
- ✦ What's the payoff?

John resists being "boxed in" by a time management system. He has tried many approaches but nothing has worked for him. He fears using a system to organize and improve his productivity won't allow him to react spontaneously. He worries it will stifle his impulsivity and creativity. As we discuss the source of this belief, he realizes it comes from his experience with other systems that were too rigid.

QUESTION YOUR BELIEFS

Once you understand the source of a belief, examine the belief for evidence that it is true in your life today. Most beliefs are stories we created to explain why certain things happened to us. For example, a child of divorced parents may believe that he's a bad person because if he'd been better, his parents would have stayed together. In fact, what really happened was simply that his parents divorced; it had nothing to do with him. Many beliefs come from what our parents, friends, culture, and church have told us, and we usually accept without question.

Patrick's homework is to look for other artists who have been able to earn a living from their creativity. I also suggest he search for careers in which his artistic abilities could allow him to support his family financially. He realizes that artists such as Picasso, Salvador Dali, Claude Monet and Michelangelo had all lived, and lived well, from their art. And today, many artists live very well from the proceeds of their art. He is also able to find several potential careers that could allow him to use his creative abilities. Now he must question his belief that to be an artist, he must "starve."

+ Does this belief reflect your current reality?
+ What is it about this belief that no longer serves you?
+ What would be possible for you if you no longer believed this limiting belief?
+ Can you find evidence that contradicts this belief?

Because he is working with his strengths, Patrick realizes he doesn't need to leave his job to be a successful artist. If he is able to be more efficient at work, finishing at 5 pm consistently, not only would he have more time to pursue his art without immediately giving up his day job, he'd also have more energy to do so.

John's homework is to investigate how other successful people, especially people he admires, manage their lives. He soon realizes that consistently using a self-management system is a common denominator. You can also use this question that really has him thinking differently:

IF ALL YOUR WORK IS COMPLETE AND YOU'VE FINISHED YOUR HOUSEHOLD CHORES, WHAT WOULD YOU DO IF YOU STILL HAD 10 MORE HOURS A WEEK TO DO ANYTHING YOU WANT?

He quickly lists a few pleasures he'd been denying himself all his life, and begins to look forward to using a self-management system that would deliver that kind of freedom.

ADOPT A NEW MORE EMPOWERING BELIEF

Your next step is to change your belief based on the new evidence you've found or change the belief to support your objectives and empower you. Patrick realizes he could live from his art if he was able to carve out time to develop it. John realizes that currently everyone else determines what he does with his time and that once he takes control of that, he can take control of his life.

ANCHOR THE NEW BELIEF WITH EVIDENCE AND ACTION

Once you shift your beliefs, you open yourself to making them real. Ask yourself,

If I believed _____ (insert your new belief here), what would be possible?

Sometimes you're not ready to accept the most ambitious belief. Patrick did not see himself becoming a full-time artist; however, he is now open to enjoying and developing his art. Acting upon it anchors this new belief.

List a few steps you can take to build evidence supporting your new belief. As you act on your new belief, things will change.

As John takes control of his agenda using *The Maximum Productivity Makeover* self-management system, he finds he has more time available for his children. He also feels more competent at work. Patrick doesn't quit his job, but he makes time to pursue his art. He no longer dismisses it; he yearns for it. You'll see more in the coming pages about how he uses other strategies to support his new belief that he could be a successful artist.

> "IF YOU THINK YOU CAN DO A THING OR YOU THINK YOU CAN'T DO A THING, YOU'RE RIGHT.
>
> HENRY FORD

Your beliefs about yourself can also hold you back. Henry Ford said, "If you think you can do a thing or you think you can't do a thing, you're right." We limit ourselves based on what others have told us about ourselves. Saying, "should" and "can't", we filter our beliefs about ourselves. Becoming aware of these filters is essential to overcome our limitations.

+ What do you truly believe about yourself?
+ IF it's negative, decide not to believe it
+ Commit to yourself and make good on those commitments
+ Celebrate each step of the way – Notice your achievements and take the time to celebrate them

HONOR THE REAL YOU
WORK WITH YOUR STRENGTHS, TALENTS AND INTERESTS

Work with your strengths, talents and interests. Your biggest potential for success comes from playing to your strengths and talents, not to your weaknesses. When faced with a weakness that is blocking your progress, look first to your strengths and talents for a solution. Otherwise, find a way to delegate or drop it. There is no potential for greatness in striving to improve your weaknesses to be "good enough." After all, the best you can become in an area of weakness is mediocre. Would you prefer to work with someone who's "the best" at something, or with someone who's "good enough."

WHEN FACED WITH A WEAKNESS THAT IS BLOCKING YOUR PROGRESS, LOOK FIRST TO YOUR STRENGTHS AND TALENTS FOR A SOLUTION.

Strengths build upon natural talent. You turn a talent into strength by acquiring skills and knowledge through practice. A talent is a naturally strong synaptic path in your brain that allows you to be especially good at certain activities. Talents are the raw material for strengths, and it is highly unlikely you'll develop an area of strength if you don't have an underlying talent.

Millions of circuits and connections make up your brain. You were born with some paths and connections stronger than others; these are talents just waiting to be discovered. Identifying and developing these talents strengthens the circuits and connections further and predispose you to greatness in these areas. Of course, to develop a talent into strength, you must be aware of what talents or strengths you have.

There are many ways to identify your strengths or talents. You can simply observe yourself, or take tests such as the *StrengthsFinder©*[1] test by the Gallup Organization. I often use the *StrengthsFinder©* test with clients who struggle to identify their strengths. Sometimes I suggest they look to their past for moments in their lives when they have felt at the top of their game.

Once you know what your strengths are, you must create a plan to develop them and integrate them in your life. Leaving it to chance does not allow you to live your best life. If you consciously take advantage of your strengths, you will begin to live your best life and achieve more success. As we'll see, each of our Creative Geniuses has talents and strengths we were able to identify together and that they were then able to exploit to improve their lives and achieve their goals. You can easily follow their example.

One of Patrick's strengths is in creating systems. While he's far from a linear thinker, a lifetime of trying to eliminate distractions combined with several years' military experience helped him develop this talent into a real strength. Together we identify areas that allow him to use this strength. He's a talented artist and also an excellent writer. As you will see later, we will work on developing his artistic talents further. Furthermore, he could use his writing abilities as a way to promote himself and his art.

Sonia is a visionary thinker who can see the "Big Picture." She uses this strength to create and communicate a compelling vision for her company. The same strengths allow her to offer her clients the added benefit of being able to pinpoint potential problems with or spot opportunities to improve their designs so they can make an informed decision. She is also very charismatic and uses this in her marketing by meeting potential clients face-to-face whenever possible.

---

[1] StrengthsFinder 2.0 by Tom Rath & Now Discover Your Strengths, Marcus Buckingham and Clifton

Finally, John's strengths include sociability and his extremely creative out-of-the-box thinking. The *StrengthsFinder©* test identified him as a Developer, someone who sees the potential in others. He already uses this strength with his sons. He's committed to doing this more effectively. Finally, he is a strategic thinker, able to see patterns where others see clutter.

VALUES

Values are those things that are important to you. When you honor your values, you feel fulfilled, authentic and fully expressed. If you go against your values, you'll feel "like a fraud." When forced to do something that goes against or disregards your values, it creates an internal conflict, which can lead to procrastination, self-sabotage or worse. For example, if honesty is one of your most important values and your work requires questionable ethics, you will feel unhappy and struggle at your job.

Our lives are very hectic so we rarely take time to think about our values. You may not even know what they are. We often talk about values in a judgmental way, saying things like, "He has poor values." However, values are neither positive nor negative; they just are. Regardless of your values, people will notice, and you will feel, the harmony and sense that this is right for you when you honor and live your values.

IDENTIFYING YOUR VALUES

It's often difficult for people to identify their values because they judge their values, sometimes rejecting a value they hold but consider bad. Even the language of values includes words such as integrity, love, dignity, justice, mastery, relating, connecting, adventure, challenge, contribution and independence. I often complete a values inventory with my clients to help them identify their values. Ask yourself:

✦ "What do I feel is important in life?"

✦ "What does success look like to me?"
✦ "What do I love the most in my life?"

Then write your response. You'll notice some values in what you write. For me success means making a contribution. For Sonia, what's important is excellence, passion and integrity, choosing to work on projects she's passionate about and where her team can deliver with excellence; for John, being connected to his boys and inspiring them is the most important thing. Patrick's guiding values include family and creating beauty, but he's been struggling with these values because he's exhausted at the end of the day so he doesn't spend much time with his kids, let alone on his art. His job drains him, leaving no energy left for his family. It's been years since he's gone out with his wife just for fun.

HONOR YOUR VALUES

You honor your values by creating a life that allows you to live them. You let nothing interfere with them and you make choices that allow you to feel authentic. When you do something that goes against your values, you feel conflicted. To identify whether you are in a values conflict, consider each value and ask yourself:

✦ When do I express this value?
✦ Are there situations where I go against this value?
✦ What changes can I make that would allow me to live this value more fully?

Patrick feels conflicted about his family value because he has created financial problems for his family and because he has no energy left for them. He decides to get some help to become more responsible financially. First, he monitors his spending each day. He carries a small notepad on which he writes every penny he spends throughout the day.

He also starts organizing dates with his wife, and taking time to talk with his children each day. Though at first, he only asks how their day was, as he re-earns their confidence in his commitment to them, he is able to increase his activities with them gradually.

Sonia realizes she often encounters clients who want to pay her "under the table" to avoid paying sales taxes. She's allowed it a few times to make her clients happy but each time the decision has weighed heavily on her conscience. She decides that in the future, if clients insist, she will simply refuse to work with them. There are other clients, and the negative impact of going against her values is not worth keeping a client or two happy.

Honoring your values provides peace and happiness in your life; meeting your needs calms "the savage beast" in you.

NEEDS ARE NOT OPTIONAL

Everyone has needs, and if your needs are not met, your quality of life suffers. Needs are those things you must have in order to be yourself and to be open to evolving. Unmet needs take over your focus at the expense of everything else.

DENYING YOUR NEEDS STOPS YOU FROM PROGRESSING.

Denying your needs stops you from progressing. Unmet needs are like a hungry baby; they cry out until you feed them. When you are upset or unhappy, ask yourself what need is not being met. We often feel guilty about meeting our needs, worried that people will consider us selfish if we meet our needs first. But until you meet your personal needs, you cannot help anyone else, so meeting your needs is far from selfish. It's the only way you'll have the fuel to help others.

37

MEETING YOUR NEEDS IS ACTUALLY FAR FROM SELFISH. IT'S THE ONLY WAY YOU'LL HAVE THE FUEL TO HELP OTHERS.

The good news is that meeting your needs is not an insurmountable challenge. You don't need to meet your needs in every aspect of your life. That is, if you have a strong need to be admired, you only need to be admired at work, at home or in your volunteer work; you don't need to be admired in all areas of your life. As you meet some needs, others may become more prevalent so needs will change and evolve over time.

Meeting your needs requires that you first be aware of them. To identify them, notice what areas of your life leave you feeling dissatisfied.

Patrick has a strong need for financial security. When he's living from paycheck to paycheck, financial security will always be an unmet need that occupies at least some, if not most, of his attention and drains his energy. He needs to find ways to meet this need. With Patrick, we work on a few strategies: he becomes more aware of his spending habits, sets up automated savings and adopts strategies to cut costs.

Sonia needs acclaim. So long as no one recognizes her achievement as a woman in (at least traditionally) a man's world, she boasts to everyone about what she's achieved. This doesn't endear her to people. She realizes that to gain this acclaim, she needs to become better known. She joins the Chamber of Commerce and volunteers to head a committee to increase the representation of women in the Chamber. Before long, she is recognized for her contribution and her charisma. As she becomes more recognized and admired, her tendency to brag disappears.

MEETING YOUR UNMET NEEDS OPENS UP POSSIBILITIES AND MAKES YOU MORE ATTRACTIVE TO OTHERS.

As you can see, unmet needs can hold you back as you consciously or unconsciously seek to fill them first. Meeting your unmet needs opens up possibilities and makes you more attractive to others.

CONCLUSION

Leaving your comfort zone is, well, uncomfortable. That's why you can easily find yourself resisting change, but there's a secret weapon you can use to overcome your resistance. Build a dream, a big dream, a dream that's outside of your comfort zone, and then create opportunities to experience that dream coming to life. Most of us don't realize we have beliefs that are holding us back, and of course, until we are aware of them, we can't even take steps to shift them. Often we're sabotaging our own efforts without even realizing it.

In addition to your transforming your limiting belief so they serve you rather than sabotage your efforts, we explored three important elements that solidify the foundation of the life you deserve:

- ✦ You will reach your true potential when you invest more effort developing your strengths and talents than you do "fixing" your weaknesses.
- ✦ Honoring your values allows you to feel authentic and fulfilled, so it's essential to notice when to identify them and to take steps to honor them.
- ✦ Finally, your unmet needs will have you waste huge amounts of energy either fulfilling them or resisting them, so take steps to fill them.

- Dreams will give you energy and motivation

- Aim higher than "normal" toward a compelling dream or goal

- Beliefs move you forward or hold you back

- Be aware of your beliefs and question your limiting beliefs

- Adopt new, more empowering beliefs

- Anchor new beliefs with evidence and action

- Meet your needs to have a quality of life

If you feel you'd like to get into action right now to build your dream, visit Succeed in a FLASH at **www.succeedinaflash.com.**

For additional information and support, visit Coach Linda Walker at **www.CoachLindaWalker.com**

PART ONE. BUILDING A SOLID FOUNDATION – CONCLUSION

In Part I, you laid the foundation for a bright future. You've identified potential points of resistance and limiting beliefs and you've taken initial steps to overcome them by building a big dream and choosing more empowering beliefs. This work will continue, of course, but we have firm ground to build on.

You also learned that because making permanent and fundamental changes in your life is your goal, it is essential to identify and develop your strengths, honor your values and to meet your unmet needs. Together, these create the cornerstone upon which you can build a life that will allow you to realize your dreams.

PART TWO
REALIZE YOUR DREAMS

CHAPTER 4
Set SMARTer Goals

CHAPTER 5
Get Motivated, Stay Motivated

CHAPTER 6
Layered Learning

CHAPTER 7
Achieve with Action

CHAPTER 8
Create the Simplest Possible Systems

CHAPTER 9
Hone Your Habits

PART TWO. REALIZE YOUR DREAMS

To make your dreams for your life a reality, you need to set and work toward objectives or goals. Without goals, working hard is no more effective at achieving progress than a hamster running on a wheel. Goals allow you to set your course and provide a point of comparison so you can tell whether you're on track, making necessary adjustments as you go.

Ambitious goals encourage you to stretch out of your comfort zone to attempt things and take actions you've never tried before. The FLASH framework, a powerful tool designed to work in concert with the Creative Genius brain, introduced in Chapter 4, is so essential to goal setting that we'll spend the remainder of Part 2 mastering the elements you'll need to achieve your goals.

CHAPTER FOUR
||||||||||||||||||||||||||||||

SET SMARTER GOALS

S uccessful people set goals and learn to motivate themselves as they strive to achieve their objectives. In this chapter, you'll learn strategies that will allow you to engage your emotional brain to keep you motivated and moving toward your goals. An emotional motive is far more compelling than logic or obligation so this strategy puts enormous power to determine your future in your hands. You'll also learn how to set the Creative Genius-adapted version of SMART goals, adjusted to work with the way your brain works, and that allow you to choose your target, zero in your sights and aim right. And finally, we'll introduce the secret weapon for Creative Geniuses who want to set and reach ambitions goals, the FLASH© framework.

THE CHANGE PROCESS

You want to change the world. Or at least, you want to change your world. We all want "things to get better," even if we haven't decided exactly how we'd like things to be if they are no longer the way they are now. John, Sonia and Patrick all want their lives to change for the better; some aspects of their lives must change dramatically, while in other areas, even small changes will bring major improvements.

Change is difficult for everyone. We resist change because we are "programmed" to behave in a certain way. Just as a wheel prefers to roll in the rut, we easily maintain the same behavior. We call it our "comfort zone." To change your life, you need to break out of your comfort zone. Remember, a rut is just like a grave with the ends kicked out.

Kurt Lewin, considered the "founder of social psychology," developed a simple three-step change model: 1) Reduce the forces that keep you in the status quo. You must acknowledge the need for change and be willing to undo what you've been doing. You likely feel uncomfortable and unstable at this stage. 2) Develop new behaviors, adjusting as you learn what works and what doesn't, but also develop new beliefs and adopt new values and attitudes, and finally, 3) "refreeze," stabilizing into a new state of equilibrium or comfort zone.

Change creates temporary instability in your life, an uncomfortable state you usually work hard to avoid. If you attempt to change too fast, or to change too many behaviors at once, your resistance will increase, as do your odds of failing. Instead, change your behavior by the smallest margin that will make a measurable difference, and then pause to stabilize the change, making the new behavior part of your normal routine. Once your new behavior moves into your comfort zone, your own resistance to change ensures you'll continue to do it.

Repeating this three-step process allows you to change your behavior any way you choose, one small modification at a time. Because you're breaking out of your comfort zone each time, each change is difficult, and if the life you want to create is ultimately very different from the one you have now, you'll make many, many changes. It sounds like hard work, and it is, although it is much more feasible using baby steps. Now you can see why, to take on this challenge, you need more motivation than simple willpower.

WILLPOWER IS A FINITE RESOURCE

You can invest some effort simply because you decide to do so. Our willpower, the power of our brains to make a decision and dictate that we follow a new behavior, is only sufficient to motivate a minor change in behavior, or to maintain the change for a short time.

Neuroscientists say we have three brains: the reptilian brain responsible for preserving life, the limbic brain that's responsible for our emotional health and the "fight or flight" process, and the neocortex which is the part of the brain that can think, decide, and reason.

This is important because even if we've made a decision to change (in our neocortex), if our emotional brain is not engaged, it will not cooperate and instead will opt for what it considers safer or more pleasing.

Change makes us feel unsure of ourselves, makes us doubt ourselves and doesn't usually feel like fun, so as soon as it feels fear or discomfort, your emotional brain will disengage. This is why it's important for your goals to be emotionally compelling, fun, new and easy.

A clear vision of how your future will be once you have made the changes you envision can be sufficiently motivating for you to accomplish anything. The real fuel to reach your goals comes from your dreams, not willpower. Picture your dream clearly in your mind, so clearly you can already feel as if you achieved it. You'll be unstoppable.

THE REAL FUEL TO REACH YOUR GOALS COMES FROM YOUR DREAMS, NOT FROM WILLPOWER.

But to make the changes that will allow you to realize that dream, you must identify specific goals that will move you in the right direction. Those goals help define the baby steps that bring you closer and closer to living your dream.

SETTING GOALS

Developing a clear vision of your dream enables you to identify the goals that will help you realize your dream. Patrick's dream is to earn his living as an artist. Closing his eyes, he imagines the day he's holding an exhibition at a downtown art gallery, greeting visitors and describing his inspiration for each piece, basking in their admiration and accepting a large check from the gallery owner after his first solo exhibit sells out.

Sonia imagines she is speaking to and inspiring a group of young women to think beyond traditional roles as women, but most importantly, to discover and work with their strengths and pursue their passions, wherever that might lead them down a career path, to take on leadership roles in their families and communities, to seek fulfillment in non-traditional careers or to consider entrepreneurship to make their mark in the world.

John closes his eyes and sees himself with his family at their country home in the woods, out of the reach of cell phones and work interruptions, canoeing with his sons on the glassy surface of the lake, watching the sun rise in the wee hours of the morning.

For each, the dream is emotionally compelling; an important factor in your dream's ability to move you out of your comfort zone.

Based on his dream, Patrick knows one of his goals is to find a gallery to represent his art and to do so he must prepare his portfolio so he can approach galleries about working with them. He also needs to make time to paint and improve his skills. Sonia knows she must set goals that will improve her business, but she must also take a more active role in her community if she hopes to make a real difference in the lives of young women by inspiring them to see beyond what others have imagined as a future for them. John sets goals to save money for the cottage's down payment and to improve his work-life balance so he can spend more time with his family.

To realize their dreams, John, Sonia and Patrick have many things to do, some of which they will enjoy, while others will be tedious at best. When tackling an interesting goal, their creative minds immediately activate, whirling with ideas, solving problems and pursuing opportunities with unstoppable energy. However, an un-interesting goal, regardless of its importance, presents an almost insurmountable obstacle.

For most people, establishing a goal as important is sufficient to ignite their brain and allow them to focus as they make progress toward achieving it. However, it's not enough for a Creative Genius. While your goal may be important, or even critical (I must get my taxes done by the April deadline or pay penalties or worse!), that doesn't make it interesting. Because you're an interest-based performer, just wanting something doesn't guarantee you'll get it done. You must ignite your brain before you can start, so you need a more effective way to spark your brain when facing goals that, though important, don't necessarily interest you.

As visionaries or "big picture" thinkers, Creative Geniuses often struggle to prioritize, classify and organize the details of a plan of action. Traditional goal setting depends on you to figure out "how" to achieve a goal. Setting a goal provides the target, but you need a systematic plan to reach that target, and standard strategies for making a plan of action don't always work with your unique way of doing things.

BE SMART BY DEFINING YOUR GOALS

Writing a clear definition of your goal will help you determine the steps to get there, and since you're working toward something positive, you're a lot more likely to achieve your goals. Feeling that you're working toward something positive rather than running away from something you don't have or don't want is very empowering. Rather than listing the things you don't have or the things you don't want to define what you need to do to achieve your goal, you'll have more success if instead, you imagine you've already achieved your goal. Close your eyes and picture yourself having accomplished your goal. Now, notice the things you have and the things you've done. Write them down, because those are the building blocks of your goals, tasks and your plan of action.

People use the "SMART" acronym to remember how to define a goal, which provides an excellent starting point, even for Creative Geniuses. Make sure your goal is:

S – Specific: Specific goals describe your result clearly enough so everyone involved knows exactly what's at stake. You don't want to "lose weight." You want to "drop three dress sizes."

M – Measurable: Make your goals measurable so you'll know when you're done. You can never reach a goal such as, "I want to be rich." But, with, "My business will have $1,000,000 in assets with less than $500,000 in debt," you'll know exactly where you stand and when you've reached your goal.

A - Action-oriented: Action-oriented goals move you forward. Dig until you find actions that are within your control and that will give the results you want. "I want my spouse to love me" is not fully under your control. Instead, if you state, "I will become a likeable, patient, and loving person," you're more likely to achieve it. Don't define your goal as, "I want to double sales." Dig deeper to define the actions you can take that will result in doubled sales; "I will increase my advertising budget by 10%, increase sales commissions by 5% and spend 3 additional hours per week meeting with prospects."

R – Realistic: Your goals should be challenging but realistic. Goals you believe are possible to achieve are motivating. Impossible goals are de-motivating. If you set impossible goals, goals you feel you'll never reach no matter how hard you work, you'll give up before you make much progress, if you make any effort at all. Remember that you move toward the realization of your dream using goals as baby-steps along the way. While your goals must be small enough to be realistic, as the source of your motivation, your dream should be as big as you can imagine.

T – Timed: Without a due date or a deadline for your goal, it's only a wish. Setting a time limit for a goal transforms that goal from "wishful thinking" into actions that yield concrete results. As a bonus, Creative Geniuses often find they're far more productive "under the gun." Setting a challenging deadline can provide the urgency that will activate your brain. When will you achieve your results?

HEADING IN THE RIGHT DIRECTION

Set goals that make you feel you're working toward something rather than running away from something. Scientific studies in Positive Psychology, shows that avoidance goals don't work as well as forward-moving goals. Want proof? Try <u>not</u> to think about something unpleasant ("I am not going to eat those cookies in the cupboard and ruin my diet.") The harder you try not to think about it, the more it consumes you. However, if you think about something pleasant instead of focusing on what you want to avoid, the unpleasant thought is less likely to come back. ("I'm going to look so good for my high school reunion, everyone will be jealous!")

SET GOALS THAT MAKE YOU FEEL YOU'RE WORKING TOWARD SOMETHING RATHER THAN RUNNING AWAY FROM SOMETHING.

Forward-moving goals drive you forward. When you work toward the things you want rather than move away from things you don't want, you have more success. John will have far more luck with a goal to get a promotion or of being more in control of his work day than he would with a goal to avoid losing his job.

Sonia increases her chances of success by setting goals to grow her business instead of simply trying to avoid losing potential sales. Patrick will make more progress working toward financial security rather than working to get out of debt. Of course, getting out of debt is part of the process, but your positive mindset has a dramatic impact.

CREATIVE GENIUSES SET GOALS

Let's examine some examples of the goals set by each of our Creative Geniuses. Note how each goal is a forward-looking SMART goal. Although we won't look at all the goals, each of them focuses on three, or occasionally four, major goals similar to the ones discussed here. Once you've achieved a goal, which can happen faster even than the deadline you set, set your next goal immediately, building momentum as you move toward the realization of your dream.

Sonia wants to increase her sales by about 40% to $1.2 million, and achieve a profit of $300,000 within the next 12 months. Last year she completed 39 projects with her two teams, but had to lay them off at times because there weren't enough projects to keep them busy all year round. She feels she can reach her sales and profit targets if she completes 55 projects this year. To do this, she has decided she will work on two key aspects of her business.

When her company completes a project, Sonia's clients are usually very happy with the results and especially with the service. Sonia ensures the worksite is clean and she follows up personally to see that the crew finished every detail. Already, she has received a number of referrals from her clients. This year, one goal is to develop a business process to ask for and follow up on referrals from satisfied customers, which Sonia feels will increase the number of prospects sufficiently to provide all the clients she needs to reach her sales target.

Sonia struggles to complete her paperwork, and she knows she lost at least eight potential clients last year because she was unable to deliver a promised proposal on time. This year, Sonia set a goal to develop a business process to ensure she delivers every proposal on time. The process has three components. She will establish rules to choose the projects for which she'll submit proposals based on her ideal client (she has wasted time preparing proposals for jobs she can't win, and for jobs she couldn't deliver profitably.) She'll use an agenda to manage her time and her proposal delivery deadlines so she no longer misses any. And she'll develop a system of proposal templates and spreadsheets that will allow her to deliver quality proposals in less than half the time it takes now.

One of Patrick's goals is to find a gallery to represent his art within two years and to build a mailing list of 500 fans and collectors by then. To approach a gallery about representing his art, Patrick knows he needs a portfolio of at least a dozen high-quality paintings, an artist's statement, curriculum vitae or C.V. and an artist's biography. Patrick's plan is to work with a professional artist who can mentor him and help him prepare his artist's statement and biography within the next 12 months. He will also add to his C.V. by exhibiting his paintings at least four times this year and six times next year.

Patrick will also paint at least one new painting each month, providing sufficient paintings to select from for his portfolio. Patrick has already sold several of his paintings to friends and neighbors, local companies and people at the local art fair, so he knows there is demand for his work. He will build a Web site to display and promote his art, create a system to collect names of visitors for his mailing list, and he will collect names from people he meets when exhibiting his paintings.

To realize his dream, John will begin saving money for the down payment for his country home. His goal is to save $5,000 this year. He also wants to become more effective and efficient at work so he can spend more time with his family. John regularly works 70 to 80 hours per week and still struggles to keep up with the demands of his colleagues. He often brings work home even though he arrived at the office early and stayed late into the night.

To better balance his work and family time, John's goal is to complete his work within 45 hours per week in the next six months. To do that, John will develop more efficient work habits so he is able to deliver his work on time, cut the hours he spends on his deliverables in half and finish work by 5 pm every evening.

Defining your goals is essential, but it isn't enough to write goals down to make your dreams come true. In the following section, we'll share a framework developed to help Creative Geniuses accomplish small and large goals with ease. Numerous Creative Geniuses just like you have used the FLASH framework successfully to transform their lives, one goal at a time.

SUCCEED IN A FLASH (ACHIEVE YOUR GOALS)

You've probably seen or even tried one or more systems people use for setting and achieving goals, more commonly known as personal productivity or time management systems. Unfortunately, these systems are often extremely complicated, and mostly are ineffective, especially for Creative Geniuses. Rather than helping, they become a hindrance as they add to your administrative load.

If you've "been there, done that," you're not alone. The problem with traditional approaches to time management is that they don't serve you. They help you serve other people. There's nothing wrong with serving other people, but you have your own goals you want to reach as well.

Traditional approaches address some issues in managing your time. They may help you remember appointments or things you've promised to do, but before long, you've filled your days with things to do and appointments to keep that don't bring you any closer to achieving your goals or realizing your dreams.

We all start with a false assumption. Try as you might, you can't manage time. Time isn't a commodity. It's not like money. If you spend less of it, or if you invest it wisely, you still won't end up with more! Nothing you do can give you more time than you have now.

To take control of your time and your life, to accomplish your goals and realize your dreams, you need a "Self-Management System." No one system can satisfy each of you, but the FLASH "framework" will let you build a system that will help you achieve your goals and reach your objectives in the best possible way for you, and so help you create the life you want.

A framework is like a building's foundation. With the right foundation, you can build a log cabin or you can build a castle. That foundation gives you the confidence that, no matter what you build on top of it, it won't tumble down around you.

The FLASH framework lays the foundation for a "Self-Management System" you can then use to build any life you desire. Apply the five simple steps of FLASH and YOU will consistently accomplish almost any goal, achieve almost any desired objective and literally change your life.

CONCLUSION

Change is difficult. Instead of relying on willpower, improve your motivation by engaging your emotional brain to support your decision to realize your goals. And it's essential to set forward-looking goals. Running away is not motivating for long. SMART goals allow you to stay focused on concrete objectives and to know when you have achieved them.

Most importantly, we introduced the FLASH framework, which will serve you well to Find your Fuel, apply Layered Learning, Achieve with Action, creating Simple Systems and Honing Habits that support you and move you toward your goals. In the remaining chapters in Part 2, we'll examine in detail how to apply the FLASH framework step-by-step to achieve your own goals and transform your life.

- ✦ The fuel to reach your goals comes from your dreams, your vision of the future, not willpower

- ✦ Set dreams that are emotionally compelling

- ✦ Define SMART goals

  - Specific results
  - Measurable so that you'll know when you've achieve them
  - Action-oriented so that they depend on action you take
  - Realistic yet challenging
  - Time-oriented with a deadline

If you feel you'd like to get into action right now to build your dream, visit Succeed in a FLASH at **www.succeedinaflash. com.**

For additional information and support, visit Coach Linda Walker at **www.CoachLindaWalker.com.**

CHAPTER FIVE
IIIIIIIIIIIIIIIIIIIIIIIIIIIIIII

GET MOTIVATED, STAY MOTIVATED

In this chapter, we'll delve deeply into the first element of the FLASH© framework. We'll see how to Find Your Fuel, identifying what motivates you to achieve the results you want to see in your life. We'll then see how you can create an "emotional charge" that acts as an energizing fuel cell for your efforts to achieve your goal, and we'll see how you can ensure you stay the course by feeding your fuel and gaining support.

Getting and staying motivated is critical, and yet this is a step Creative Geniuses often skip in your eagerness to get started. You impulsively jump into action. Excited by a new idea or challenge, it's difficult to pause and consider what you'll use to refuel your resolve down the road. Starting out, you're enthusiastic but that won't always be the case. It's hard work to fight against your resistance to change, so you'll be tempted to return to the status quo. You must remember what you're aiming for at every step or you won't have the staying power to reach the finish line.

FIND YOUR FUEL

Your dream, the fuel that takes over when that initial burst of enthusiasm and willpower give out, is so important that it's the first thing I look for when clients tell me what they'd like to achieve during our coaching. You must know the source of your fuel, of your motivation and you must be able to tap into that fuel whenever you need a shot of energy to keep going. As we continue, we'll see ways for you to draw on your fuel supply whenever you need it.

Without a compelling dream, as soon as you hit a snag, you won't be able to continue. You'll be tempted to slide right back into your comfort zone. People suffer from obesity, find themselves in financial trouble or struggle to stay organized, not because they lack desire. They WANT to lose weight, to improve their finances, to be organized, but they don't have the fuel to take action and to keep taking steps in the right direction until the change is complete and permanent. If you forget, even for a minute, why you're making this effort, or if the reason isn't compelling enough, you'll lack the motivation to keep going and will quickly slip backwards. A powerful dream is like having a rope you can grab onto to keep from sliding back, while you catch your breath for another sprint forward.

WITHOUT A COMPELLING DREAM, AS SOON AS YOU HIT A SNAG, YOU WON'T BE ABLE TO CONTINUE.

The FLASH framework has one limitation; it will only work for goals YOU want to achieve. It's not enough that your spouse wants you to be organized. It's not enough that your boss wants you to be on time. If someone else is choosing your goals, save your energy. In fact, "should" is a clue that indicates a goal is not really your goal. If you set a goal for something you "should" do, you're giving in to someone else's influence rather than focusing on your own desires. Since you're the one doing the work, it's unlikely you'll be able to achieve a goal simply to please someone else.

Change is challenging. If it were easy, we would all be at our ideal weight, have a ton of money, pursue the career of our dreams and live a healthy, stress-free lifestyle. Most people believe the adage, "Better the devil you know." The unknown is so uncomfortable they choose to stay in a rut even if it prevents them from realizing their dreams, even if the status quo risks their health and ultimately their life simply because it is easier.

Escaping the rut requires effort, yes, but even more, it demands faith, faith that you can do what you've set out to do, faith that it will work for you, faith that you'll realize the benefits you anticipate and faith that you'll be happier once you make the change. That's a lot of faith!

Your fuel, your dream, reinforces your faith that the destination is worth it. The more real you can paint the pictures of your dream realized in your imagination, the more motivating it will be and the more powerful your faith. Finding your fuel includes:

+ Identifying what motivates you to change,
+ Finding evidence that it can happen, and
+ Creating a way of continually reigniting that fuel as you move forward.

What is your passion? What do you love to experience, talk about and learn more about? I can often identify a client's passion just by listening. When discussing your passion, you speak faster, become more animated and more focused.

Igniting and re-igniting your passion with the right fuel helps you overcome procrastination, recharge your flagging energy and focus like a laser. What is your dream? Can you visualize a better tomorrow? Are you emotional about it?

IGNITING AND RE-IGNITING YOUR PASSION WITH THE RIGHT FUEL HELPS YOU OVERCOME PROCRASTINATION, RECHARGE YOUR FLAGGING ENERGY AND FOCUS.

You may want to lose weight because you want to look good but unless you associate that objective with the emotional reason to be around to see your kids grow up – like Patrick's dream – you won't have the fuel you need to keep you going.

Creative Geniuses have a significant advantage once they learn that the key to successfully reach their goals is to develop a compelling dream. Many people find it extremely challenging to create a gripping vision of their future, but then they don't have your creativity and imagination.

Are you feeling emotional about your goal? If not, take the time to write down at least 20 to 40 reasons – 200 is better - why it's important to you to achieve the goal. At some point you'll put your finger on that emotional, compelling reason that will drive you to success.

Sonia dreams of being a role model to young girls to not allow gender dictate what career they'll do, even in a non-traditional industry. She dreams of being a positive role model for her daughter and for all women. To feed her fuel, she wrote a detailed story about her interview for a future magazine article. Though it was fiction, she imagined how it would happen in such detail that she could feel her pride and the respect and admiration she will enjoy when the article appears in a national magazine. Of course, another source of motivation is having the time to be with her kids and to travel once she begins recruiting franchisees.

FEEL YOUR FUEL

Nothing makes an experience more real than creating that feeling in your gut of how it will be once you get there. Rather than focusing on your current circumstances, you want to feel the passion and excitement of achieving your goals and realizing your dreams.

It may be difficult for you to feel the emotions associated with experiencing your dream if you've never lived it, but there are ways to make the experience more real for you. Many activities can help you find and feel your fuel:

- ✦ Taste-test the lifestyle you'll enjoy once you've achieved your goal. Test-drive the car you want. Visit open houses. Borrow or rent a cottage for a weekend.
- ✦ Dress the part, act the part. Do a dress rehearsal of your own successful dream. If you want to be a renowned professor, wear a tweed blazer with leather patches on the elbows. Future successful entrepreneurs and executives, wear your best suit, even when you're going to work in your home office.

ACT AS IF...

You'll reinforce your dream when you dress and act as the person you want to become instead of who you are right now. Acting "as if" means creating a body environment, a physical environment and a network environment that supports what you are trying to accomplish.

Patrick struggles with his weight. After numerous failed attempts to lose weight following strict diets, Patrick was so discouraged he thought "bad genes" meant no matter how hard he tried, he'd never reach a healthy weight. His weight had been out of control so long, he'd been diagnosed with Type II diabetes. Luckily, this prompted a meeting with a dietician who informed him he didn't need any temporary measures like diets. He would always be a diabetic so he needed to adopt a different, healthier lifestyle instead.

Patrick realized that rather than try to lose weight, he needed to shift his thinking. If he was to become a healthy man, he must act as if he were already a healthy man. When choosing food or activities, he must ask, "What would a thin healthy man like me do in this case? Would a healthy man go for a walk or watch TV?

Would a healthy man like me choose an apple or a piece of pie for desert?" This was a first but most important step on his quest for better health.

One of the most powerful ways of acting "as if" is to express your gratitude for having already received what you want to achieve. Nothing strengthens your faith like showing gratitude for all you have received, even before you receive it, as if it was already yours.

Patrick applies the same techniques by acting "as if" he's a professional artist. He visits several art galleries to choose the ones where he would display his paintings. Once he selects his favorites, he visits their Web sites to find photos of their exhibition space. He downloads them and "Photoshops" his paintings in place of the ones displayed. He writes a card preparing the speech he'll give at the gallery, "I'm so happy you could all come this evening, and I'm very grateful to the gallery for putting on this exhibition, my first solo exhibition." He keeps the picture where he can see it and practices his speech frequently. It constantly motivates him so that while he might prefer to sleep in on Saturday morning after a long workweek, he gets up early to paint because that's what a professional artist with commitments to galleries and eager fans awaiting his new work would do.

If you have trouble imagining what your life will be like once you've achieved your objectives, interview someone who's already achieved the dream you're pursuing. Ask them about their life, and especially ask about how it feels to live as they do.

FEED YOUR FUEL

Whatever your dream, always keep it active in your mind. Once you find your passion, developing your dream and keeping it alive requires effort; you can't just think about it once. There will be times you're tempted to quit, so take the time to anchor the dream in your heart. Hold your dream in front of you so that when you're tempted to quit, you'll have a reserve of fuel you can draw on to re-energize you, and keep your dream alive using visual, auditory and kinetic reminders.

When I worked as a project manager, one project was severely underfunded and I constantly struggled to make any progress. When I felt like quitting, I was able to use my vision for the project outcome to motivate the team to continue despite major obstacles. I believed the successful implementation of this project would revolutionize the way the company interacted with and served clients and become an important tool for our sales force. I chose a favorite tune as the project's theme song and I would play it often to celebrate even small victories.

Later, if things weren't going as well or when I felt discouraged, I could listen to "Right Here, Right Now" by Jesus Jones and let the music remind me of past victories and make me feel there would be future victories as well. I created a shortcut to the digital song recording on my computer desktop and when things got ugly, I'd play the song to re-energize my team and myself.

Find music or pictures that re-energize you. As a Creative Genius, use your own talents to create a collage or vision board of what you want, or draw or paint something that represents it. Music and rhythm strikes a primal chord in our brain. Find music that stimulates your spirit or create a dance that makes you feel like a winner. If you're musically talented, you can even write and record a song you can play to refuel you as you strive to reach your goals.

In the movie, "Remember the Titans," the football team used a dance to pump themselves up. We often see football players do a quirky dance after they make a touchdown; successful players often practice their dance long before they ever score their first touchdown. This dream building fuels them through the hard work of practices and mental preparation. They're motivated to do whatever it takes, all for chance to do the dance in front of a cheering crowd.

John chooses to enlist his kids' help to build his dream and keep it in front of him. Together, they're planning their next vacation; they'll "test-drive" a cottage in the country. John takes time at least once a week to talk to his children about the vacation. He tells them stories about the fun things he did as a child when his parents took him to a cottage and he solicits their ideas of things they'd like to try. Would they like to go fishing? Would they enjoy canoeing? He even assigns them "research projects" to investigate potential activities they would all enjoy.

John's approach has some added benefits as well. By doing this, he's already spending extra time with his children, building the dream for himself and for them at the same time. He's also creating especially powerful fuel for any parent. He wants his children to be happy and he's showing them what is possible when you build dreams and set goals, and he's even more motivated to work toward his goals so he won't disappoint his kids.

Here are a few more ideas you can use to help you "feed the fuel":

+ Write a newspaper announcement about your accomplishment.
+ Record an interview with yourself. Play the parts of the interviewer and the interviewee, asking about how you achieved your amazing success, and answer as if you had already achieved it.
+ Create a dance you use to celebrate or to boost your spirits.
+ Write a mantra or affirmation you recite every day.

ACCESS USEFUL SUPPORT

Your environment – physical, financial, network, social, family, etc. – either supports you or keeps you from progressing. The most challenging to control is your family environment. You need positive input. Often your family and friends won't support or even understand your desire for a better life. Your desire for a better life calls into question their willingness to settle for the life they have, and it's far easier for them to discourage you from changing than it is for them to make the effort to change their own lives.

You improve your odds of success when you spend less time with negative people. Instead, find support where people who are trying to realize similar dreams gather. Positive support groups exist for people who want to exercise, lose weight, improve their social lives, improve their finances, create art or start a business. Visit *Meetup* (www.meetup.com) for ideas of the groups you might find (or start!) in your neighborhood. Even if a group is not officially a "support group," like-minded people who share similar dreams and goals typically offer support and encouragement, and are seeking the same from you.

Positive support groups provide help when you need it and also allow you to offer help to people who aren't as advanced in some areas as you are. When you're discouraged and wondering if you really are making progress toward your goals, it's very uplifting to help people trying to reach similar goals, especially if they aren't as advanced as you are. They appreciate your expertise and provide an excellent reminder that you were once where they are. This proves to yourself that you've made progress and shows them that achieving your goal is possible.

A word of warning: some groups devolve into "pity parties," where group members use meetings as opportunities to complain about similar challenges. Avoid such groups at all costs.

Patrick has enlisted the support of fellow artists working to become self-supporting by finding a Meetup group dedicated to working through "*The Artist's Way*," a classic book by Julia Cameron that guides Creative Geniuses to re-discover their true creative nature and to "fight back" against the drag the daily grind can put on your dreams. He's also found a local weekly workshop where fellow artist's gather to paint, critic each other's work and offer words of encouragement. This has the added benefit of "forcing" him to make extra time for painting.

Sonia joins *Toastmasters* (www.toastmasters.org) as a way to prepare for the day she'll have to give her speech but also to gain the support of forward-moving people who are ready to step out of their comfort zone.

CONCLUSION

Often overlooked, getting and staying motivated is an essential part of any objective; in fact, it is probably the single most important factor that will determine your success. Knowing that only 10% of people who purchase a book read beyond the first chapter, we realize it's rarely the difficulty of reaching an objective that causes us to abandon the effort; it's a lack of motivation. Identifying what motivates you to change, finding evidence that it can happen, getting emotional about the possibilities and creating ways to continuously reignite that fuel motivates you much more effectively than willpower.

Often, when we imagine a bright future, we're discouraged by the many things we don't know how we'll do because we've never done them before. When we know how to do something, setting it as a goal doesn't require stretching outside our comfort zone, but when we face tasks we've never attempted before, it's easy to give up before we start. In the next chapter, we'll reveal Layered Learning as a new approach to tackling more ambitious goals, goals that take you into the unknown.

- ✦ Without a compelling dream, as you hit an obstacle, you're more likely to give up

- ✦ Make sure they are goals YOU want to achieve

- ✦ Find your fuel by

  - Identifying what motivates you to change
  - Finding evidence that it can happen
  - Creating a trigger to reignite that fuel

- ✦ Feel the fuel by

  - Taste testing the outcome
  - Dressing and acting the part

- ✦ Feed your fuel

  - Keep your vision alive
  - Replenish every day by revisiting it

- ✦ Tap into positive input and support

If you feel you'd like to get into action right now to build your dream, visit Succeed in a FLASH at **www.succeedinaflash. com.**

For additional information and support, visit Coach Linda Walker at **www.CoachLindaWalker.com.**

CHAPTER SIX

||||||||||||||||||||||||||||||

PRACTICE LAYERED LEARNING

The "L" in FLASH represents Layered Learning. In this chapter, we'll explore this second element in the FLASH framework in depth. Any objective or goal you strive for will demand that you learn new behavior, even if you're very familiar with many or even most of the elements required to achieve this goal, if it warrants setting a goal, then there will be parts you've never done before. As your confidence grows and you set ever more ambitious goals, your forays into the unknown will become ever more adventurous.

Layered Learning goes beyond acquiring information. When you put into practice some small but significant tactic, technique or strategy and move from understanding a concept to a much more powerful deep-seated knowing, enabling you to potentiate your learning.

Learning is an essential component of every change, but it presents its own challenges. Learning really occurs when there is a change in behavior that accompanies the intellectual process of acquiring new information. When attempting anything for the first time, you need to learn new things. If you have nothing to learn, you're not challenging yourself. Sticking with what you know is no way to reach your goal.

Many Creative Geniuses are plagued with a history of failures. Usually, this is not because you aren't capable, but rather, because you didn't realize you were a Creative Genius! You've been working in ways that aren't how you work best; they don't fit the way your brain works. However, failure isn't pleasant so in an attempt to avoid it in the future, you may be tempted to learn everything you can about something before you try it. You're hoping to become an expert before making your first attempt to put it in practice. While you might hope to make progress without failing, it's impossible to know everything there is to know about any subject. Being an expert in any area is a never-ending task.

This approach also precludes experiential learning. Practice anchors your learning, not just in your conscious mind, but also in your subconscious. This "deep-knowing" you feel when you've learned something by practicing it, is far more powerful than anything you learn through reading, listening to someone explain something or even by watching a demonstration. You may believe you can do something, but actually doing it builds confidence impossible to achieve any other way. Until you attempt something, you can never know with certainty that you're able to do it.

TRUE LEARNING RARELY HAPPENS IN THE CLASSROOM.

True learning rarely happens in the classroom. School provides seeds for future learning; reading, attending lectures and seminars, meeting new people and observing their practices also contribute. However, time for reflection and attempting to put what you've observed into practice are essential for learning. You learn when you're doing something new or doing what you've done before in a different way.

Layered learning comes naturally to Creative Geniuses. It allows you to start immediately, overcoming any desire to procrastinate due to perfectionism and results in more effective learning. Layered learning means exactly what you think it means; learn a little, try it, practice it, learn from the practice, adjust and then learn a little bit more.

But what if it doesn't work? When you're working toward a goal, forward motion is progress. As long as you're moving in the right direction, even when you make a mistake, you're advancing. And the best way to tell if you're moving in the wrong direction is to take action and see what happens. Remember, it's impossible to steer a parked car. Get your car moving, even in the wrong direction, and you can easily turn it around and point it the right way.

FAILURE IS SIMPLY ONE APPROACH TO LEARNING.

Don't fear failure. Failure is simply one approach to learning; in fact, it's such an effective approach, most successful people use it themselves and recommend it to others. Mastery is impossible without making mistakes. Michael Jordan became the best basketball player of all time by missing many baskets. How successful would he have been if he'd never attempted a shot at the basket until he was sure he couldn't miss! Wayne Gretsky says, "You miss 100% of the shots you don't take." Take your shots and learn how you can improve them. Even the smallest lesson will make your next attempt even better. Reap the benefits, adjust and start again.

To practice Layered Learning, set your goal and identify the smallest possible action you can take that will make a significant difference. If you dream of living a healthy lifestyle, and, like Patrick, one of your goals is to develop and follow an exercise program, don't make your first step paying a small fortune for an annual gym membership. Do you think doling out that much cash will motivate you to go to the gym?

Instead, do one push up. If you're feeling energetic, do two. Whatever your first step is (but make it significant – putting on your runners isn't significant because it's not actually exercise), make it so easy that you can't possibly talk yourself out of doing it. It would probably be easier to do one push up than to convince yourself you don't have time! Learn how to do the pushup properly, without hurting yourself. Then do one push up every day. Soon it'll be so easy that you'll forget and do two, or five. Before long, you'll feel better, you'll be in better shape, and you'll feel successful.

Practice Layered Learning with the following steps:

1. Learn just enough to identify the next step or two (you don't need to know all the steps before you start!).
2. Practice what you've learned by putting it into action.
3. Step back to see what worked, what didn't and what you've learned from the practice.
4. Adjust and practice again.
5. Return to Step 1 and repeat as necessary.

Sonia, our aspiring-to-be-inspiring entrepreneur, lists the characteristics of her ideal client. This list forms the backbone of a checklist she'll use to decide which requests for proposal she should respond to so that she only invests time and energy responding to request for proposals she has a good chance of winning and where the job is one she'll be able to deliver profitably.

Patrick realizes he'll never earn his wife's support for his painting career unless he is able to support her more at home. Patrick's disorganization leaves his wife feeling as if she has an extra child at home rather than a partner to share her workload. Patrick collaborates with his wife to figure out how they can better split the household chores, so she'll also have time for herself, and so he can paint without feeling guilty or facing her resentment.

Patrick also begins to exercise. At over 300 lbs., he doesn't feel comfortable joining a gym. Instead, he starts slowly, taking stairs instead of the elevator at work. At first, he's out of breath by the third floor, and he takes the elevator the rest of the way. As his stamina increases, soon he walks easily up the six flights of stairs to his office. He soon adds walking to work, until that also becomes too easy.

Had Patrick joined a gym right away, he would have abandoned exercise quickly as too difficult. Increasing his exercise intensity slowly allowed him to build endurance and lose weight until he was ready to go to the gym. Now, he works out every day, either at the gym or swimming laps in the pool.

Identifying small steps and building on each as his body became accustomed to the effort allowed Patrick to lose over 100 lbs. Yes, it took almost two years to reach his goal weight, but he'd been struggling to do this for over a decade, reading everything he could find about exercise and diet, but he either never acted on what he learned, or he took such radical steps that he soon abandoned the effort because they were simply too difficult.

John, with his sights set on spending more time with his family, decides he needs to improve the use of his time and identifies as his first step to purchase and carry an electronic agenda. He discovers this is a little more complicated than he anticipated, as he must select a model that meets his needs and that the computer department at work supports. He knows he must synchronize his "Personal Digital Assistant" or PDA with his agenda at work, so he must choose one that is compatible with corporate standards. John also enrolls in *The Maximum Productivity Makeover* coaching program as a way to support reaching his objectives.

When Sonya first started her business, she was able to handle almost all the tasks she needed to complete regularly. Though everything was new, she had experience managing an office, and her business was still small. Today, with a goal of reaching over

$1 million in sales, she needs to focus more on drumming up business. A first step is for her to separate tasks into groups: those she enjoys or that play to her strengths, and those she dislikes or tends to procrastinate. It is the second group she'll eventually delegate, but in the coming chapters, we'll see effective ways to deal with those tasks even if you don't have a large staff just waiting to take the tasks you don't enjoy.

CONCLUSION

Creative Geniuses learn best by doing and experiencing. When you try something, if it doesn't work, you did not fail; you've learned a valuable lesson that will guide you to be more effective as you take your next steps.

Instead of waiting until you have all the answers before you move forward, implement what you've learned immediately. As soon as you've learned one new tactic, strategy or approach, identify the smallest possible action you can take that will allow you to make significant, measurable progress toward your goal and try it. Then, take a step back and evaluate what worked and what could use improving. You'll learn valuable new lessons from this practice that you can use to adjust and improve your approach. Now, identify the next step and repeat this process.

Layered Learning and Achieve with Action are two steps that work in concert. As soon as you've identified the next steps to take to progress in your projects or in achieving your goals, it's time to take action.

- ✦ Setting time for reflection and putting it into practice is essential to learning

- ✦ Layered learning allows you to start immediately and to deepen your learning as you progress toward your goal

- ✦ Failure is one approach to learning

- ✦ Identify the smallest possible action you can take that will make a significant difference

If you feel you'd like to get into action right now to build your dream, visit Succeed in a FLASH at **www.succeedinaflash. com.**

For additional information and support, visit Coach Linda Walker at **www.CoachLindaWalker.com.**

CHAPTER SEVEN
||||||||||||||||||||||||||||||||||||

ACHIEVE WITH ACTION

You accomplish your goals by taking action. As Jerry Baden, one of the top coaches with the Landmark Education Group (www.landmarkeducation.com) says, "Action gets you results; thinking only gets you thoughts!" In this chapter, we'll explore the importance of taking action, even when you don't have all the answers. Of course, that means you're going to need to be open to the possibility of taking risks.

Achieve with Action goes hand in hand with Layered Learning. You Achieve with Action when you implement what you have learned, but you also learn more each time you put a new behavior into practice. Layered Learning and Achieve with Action together form a loop that steadily increases your expertise and mastery while advancing you toward your goals.

Remember that Achieve with Action comes AFTER Layered Learning. Reaching a goal demands change. If you continue to act as you always have, change is impossible. While you cannot achieve WITHOUT action, you cannot impulsively act without learning how you should change what you're doing and expect to make progress.

Many Creative Geniuses become stuck in learning mode because they're afraid to take action, while others face what I call an implementation gap. Knowing what to do, wanting to do it, even having a plan for when and how to do it does not necessarily ensure you'll do it because you get distracted from your course of action or from procrastination. In the coming sections, we'll see ways to overcome this implementation gap.

THE BEST WAY TO ADVANCE IS TO TRY SOMETHING, STEP BACK TO SEE WHAT YOU'VE LEARNED, ADJUST AND TACKLE IT AGAIN.

The best way to advance is to try something, step back to see what you've learned, adjust and tackle it again. The average entrepreneur finally succeeds at their sixth business. Sonia, as is the case for most entrepreneurs, has had businesses fail. In fact, she failed just as often as she succeeded. She treats each failure as a learning experience so that rather than making her "gun shy," her failures make her stronger. As a serial entrepreneur myself, I can relate. I am a successful entrepreneur today because of the lessons I've learned from past failures. Even in my successful businesses, I learned the most valuable lessons from my failed projects.

As you look at your own experiences, as hard as they seemed at the time, you've learned your most valuable lessons from the struggles you've faced. To succeed more, you don't need to fear or even avoid failure; you only need to fail faster!

Ask yourself the following questions to evaluate your progress and extract the valuable lessons that will make your next step more successful and pave the way to achieving your goals.

- ✦ Would I consider this a success or a mistake, or something in between?
- ✦ What did I learn from making this step?
- ✦ How will I use what I learned in the future?
- ✦ What will I need to adjust? What steps will I take next?

Adopting a learner's posture allows you to see "failures" as learning opportunities that allow you to "build muscle" the same way you did when you learned to walk.

It also helps you to look forward to your next learning opportunity instead of avoiding the unknown. When the steps you take don't lead to the results you expect, you discover what doesn't work and you adjust to make the next step more effective.

Repetitive steps help reach your goals, but they can be boring and a source of problems for Creative Geniuses who thrive on novelty but lose interest on repetitive tasks. The next chapter helps with strategies to overcome this challenge.

CONCLUSION

To accomplish your goals, you must take action. Pairing Layered Learning with Achieve with Action allows you to try something, evaluate the results and apply what you've learned to increase your effectiveness. This continuous-improvement approach will produce results far more quickly than waiting for all the lights to turn green before starting your journey. Using it avoids common pitfalls such as procrastination, perfectionism and opens you to learning through experience so that failure is no longer devastating but simply an opportunity to improve.

||||||||||||||||||||||||||
KEY POINTS

✦ Act after learning what next step will allow you to progress in your goals

✦ Take a step back, adjust if needed, and move to the next step

✦ Adopt a learner's posture to see "failures" as learning opportunities

If you feel you'd like to get into action right now to build your dream, visit Succeed in a FLASH at **www.succeedinaflash. com.**

For additional information and support, visit Coach Linda Walker at **www.CoachLindaWalker.com.**

CHAPTER EIGHT
||||||||||||||||||||||||||||||||||

CREATE THE SIMPLEST POSSIBLE SYSTEM

Many of the steps you'll take to reach your goals are repetitive, such as exercising, using an agenda to manage your schedule or working with templates to prepare proposals more efficiently. These are all repetitive, potentially uninspiring, even boring activities our heroes face. Systems can help you continue these activities despite such hurdles.

In this chapter, we'll delve into the fourth element of the FLASH© framework, where you'll learn to create and use systems to support you in achieving your objectives, to conquer boredom and to free your time to allow you to be more creative. We'll also identify the types of activities that lend themselves well to systemization so you can begin immediately to implement changes that will improve your productivity dramatically.

It's easy for life to distract you from your objectives. Regardless of how prepared you are, things happen unexpectedly and you must deal with them. However, systems can help you ensure that your progress towards your goals doesn't slow. Without systems in place, "emergencies" happen frequently, and those emergencies cut into the activities moving us toward our goals rather than interfering with our favorite TV shows.

Systems provide an extremely powerful way to:

+ Streamline things you do repetitively,
+ Ease the strain on your memory,
+ Free up time to allow you to do more of what you enjoy and want to do,

+ Conquer boredom, and
+ Delegate when you're ready.

Creative Geniuses share their distaste for conformity. "Systems" include structures, procedures, checklists and tools you use to support your efforts to achieve the results you desire, but upon hearing the word "system" or "structure," many Creative Geniuses' eyes glaze over. Systems are boring! You resist systems because you fear they will take away your spontaneity and creativity, "boxing you in." In my experience most Creative Geniuses resist any notion of routines and systems imposing structure in their lives! Your non-conformity is one of the reasons I enjoy working with you so much, but productivity and structure go hand in hand.

You equate systems with bureaucracy and loss of creativity, but knee-jerk resistance to all structure is as harmful as an inflexible follow-the-rules-even-when-they-make-no-sense bureaucrat mentality. Yes, rigid systems can be restrictive, but a complete lack of structure is chaos. When I first meet them, most of my Creative Genius clients do not wear a watch or use an agenda, fearing this will stifle their creativity, but I know that structure enhances creativity! Without structure, too much of your time and energy is expended on the little things we all need to do, often every day.

Structure actually allows you to be MORE creative, as long as it is your own structure. You developed your resistance to structure when parents, teachers, coaches and other people tried to get you to do things their way instead of allowing you to discover the way that works best for you. When their way didn't deliver the results you needed, their justification, "But everybody does it this way!" planted the seed. You obviously weren't like everyone else, so you'd go your own way. A non-conformist is born!

STRUCTURE ACTUALLY ALLOWS YOU TO BE MORE CREATIVE,
AS LONG AS IT IS YOUR OWN STRUCTURE.

As a teenager, rebelliousness is expected, and in college, you're supposed to question the wisdom of your predecessors. However, as an adult, to accomplish your goals, you need structure that works with you instead of against you. I know you imagine your non-conformity has helped you succeed, but non-conformity is not the same as creativity. Establishing routines and systems that help you accomplish your goals will not rob you of your Creative Genius. Strangely, quite the opposite occurs when you create and implement systems to support you.

Patrick, our artist, has been hoping to find some free time to devote to painting. Though he struggles to improve his efficiency, he never has time left over to paint. Appreciating the effort Patrick made to improve his performance at work and to help around the house, Patrick's wife surprises him with a gift. She registers him for a Saturday morning painting class, essentially creating a system for him. He doesn't think he'll have time to go, but a regular appointment is a very compelling system. Somehow, he manages to make time for his art classes.

ACTIVITIES TO USE WITH SYSTEMS

Which activities are the best candidates to handle with a system or a routine? Analyzing activities in your life will let you identify the easiest ones to create systems for so that doing them can become "automatic" through established behavior patterns and routines.

Some of the characteristics of tasks for which you can create systems and easily turn into routines include:

◆ Tasks requiring little or no thought or creativity (mowing the lawn)

- ✦ Tasks with a large physical component (working out)
- ✦ Tasks requiring little or no mental energy (washing dishes)
- ✦ Tasks that don't require much time (tying your shoes)
- ✦ Tasks you have little or no interest in (folding clean laundry)
- ✦ Activities that require many steps (baking cake - in fact, recipes are systems!)

Creating a system is simple. All you need is a little time to think it through and enough creativity to design a system that will serve you well. Follow these steps:

1. Identify and state the problem clearly. (You throw your dirty clothes on the floor.)
2. Clarify the desired outcome. (You want to throw your dirty clothes in the hamper.)
3. What do you already do that could be part of the solution? (You throw your dirty clothes over the door into the corner, imagining you're a basketball star!)
4. Brainstorm alternative approaches or solutions. (You could learn to live with dirty clothes on the floor – your spouse vetoes this option, you could hire a butler to pick up after you – this would eat into your vacation fund, you could put the hamper behind the door – we have a winner!)
5. "Document" your system. (Tell everyone the clothes hamper now goes behind the door.)
6. How can you simplify or automate it? (Tape a target on the wall above the door so clothes are sure to end up in the hamper.)
7. Once you've created your system, apply the Layered Learning and Achieve with Action cycle to:
    a) Apply the system.
    b) Evaluate the results.
    c) Adjust to improve results.

John wants to save money for the down payment on a cottage, and he knows that saving the money left at the end of the month never works. There's never any left over! He must pay himself first, putting away the money for the cottage before he pays his bills, and he must "hide" the money so it's not easy to get to in emergencies. He knows that the easier it is to access the money, the more likely it is there will be an "emergency." John opens a bank account at a bank he doesn't usually visit and sets up an automated system to take money from his paycheck and deposit it in his savings account.

Sonia creates a template to help prepare proposals. She notices that certain elements of the proposal are always the same (the payment arrangements, the legal small print) and that certain types of renovations are quite similar, for example, she usually only renovates a bathroom using one of two approaches: 1) gutting the bathroom and starting fresh, or 2) a targeted approach changing only predefined items.

By standardizing descriptions whenever possible and creating several template models for the most common types of jobs, she is quickly able to develop a complete system of templates that dramatically cut the time required to prepare proposals immediately, and she has already spotted a few more potential improvements.

Systems eliminate time wasted delaying or avoiding tasks you find difficult, complex or boring. They also cut the time you spend "re-deciding" how to do the task, particularly for complex, multi-step tasks.

SYSTEMS ELIMINATE TIME WASTED DELAYING OR AVOIDING TASKS YOU FIND DIFFICULT, COMPLEX OR BORING.

Starting out in my own business, I wrote an email to every prospect who inquired about coaching. This proved time-consuming and inefficient. Many people never responded, and it took time away from clients who did want my help. Since the same questions reappeared frequently, I prepared a template to copy and paste into my email. The same emails I dreaded so much that I would put them off and work late to finish (they could take 30 to 45 minutes each!) now take less than 3 minutes, and I am still able to offer the same high level service I always did.

To help out at home, Patrick decides to take over the food shopping because his wife finds it exhausting. He creates a system in which he prepares the menu for the week, makes the shopping list based on the menu and always follows the aisles in the same pattern at the food store.

Once Patrick decides to exercise more than is possible walking to work or climbing the stairs to his office, he decides to join a gym that is on the way to work in the morning. While his resolve is strong, he frequently has to abort his plans because he miscalculates the time required to get ready for the gym in the morning, or he arrives at the gym only to discover he's forgotten his runners or the clothes he planned to change into for work.

Patrick needs a system to ensure he'll arrive at the gym with everything he needs to exercise, shower, groom and dress for work. He begins to develop a system for getting to the gym, and using Layered Learning and Achieving with Action, he works to smooth out the bumps in the road that had been stopping his workouts.

The first time he arrives at the gym too late to work out, he decides to get up earlier in the morning and be more effective with his time. Once he manages to get to the gym on time, he finds he still forgets things, so he creates a checklist for his gym clothes and his work clothes as well as his grooming supplies (i.e. shampoo, towel, deodorant and so on). These he packs the night before using his list.

CONCLUSION

When you begin developing your own systems to manage re-petitive, boring or multi-step processes, not only will you ease the strain on your memory but you'll free up more time to do what you really want to do, conquer boredom and eventually, when your business grows or when money is available, you'll delegate more easily.

Most successful people are successful because of their habits. Systems used over and over become habits, the subject of our next chapter.

✦ Systems allow you to abandon your fire fighter mode and become proactive

✦ Systems streamline boring repetitive activities, ease your memory, free up time, conquer boredom, and allow you to delegate

✦ Systems allow you more time to be creative

✦ Systemize

- Activities that require little or no thought
- Activities with a large physical component
- Activities that don't require much time
- Activities that have little or no interest to you
- Activities that require many steps

✦ To create a system:

- Identify and state the problem clearly
- Clarify the desired outcome
- What are you doing that could be part of the solution?
- Brainstorm alternative approaches
- Document your system
- Simplify and automate it

✦ Apply layered learning and achieving with action and adjust as needed.

If you feel ready to implement system in your life now but would like more in-depth explanations and support, visit Succeed in a FLASH at **www.succeedinaflash.com**.

For additional information and support, visit Coach Linda Walker at **www.CoachLindaWalker.com**

CHAPTER NINE
IIIIIIIIIIIIIIIIIIIIIIIIIIIIII

HONE YOUR HABITS

The last piece of the FLASH framework is Hone Your Habits. Habits are actions you take unconsciously, such as brushing your teeth or turning on the TV as soon as you get home. You do them without thinking, often not even realizing you're doing them or that you've done them. Have you ever wondered if you had brushed your teeth, but when you check your breath, you realize that indeed you did?

In this chapter, we'll discover how habits can help you progress toward your goals almost effortlessly, provided you choose the right habits. We'll examine effective ways to build and hone new habits to support your efforts, and we'll also see how you can eliminate habits that may not be serving you.

> "WE ARE WHAT WE REPEATEDLY DO – EXCELLENCE, THEN, IS NOT AN ACT, BUT A HABIT"
>
> ARISTOTLE

Habits are very powerful and serve either to move you toward your goals or away from them. Using effective habits, you can accomplish almost any goal with what will seem like very little effort. In FLASH, we focus on creating good habits that move you toward your goals, but you can also use it to help you change bad habits. One of the best ways to get rid of a bad habit is to replace it with a good habit.

Our brain creates stronger circuits that have us doing the same things over and over again. These paths are difficult to break. This is why we revert back to old habits so easily. Creating new habits requires creating new circuit paths, once believed to take between 21 or 30 days is now believed to take between six and eight months. So you must be determined to create new habits and to really want the results. The good news is that once we form new paths, they also tend to become difficult to change.

You need a strong desire and to be persistent. It's also important to consider what need you are meeting with the old habit. Patrick's habit of raiding the refrigerator met his need for comfort from the chaos in his life. One of Sonia's bad habits is to buys things for her children to ease her guilt about working too long.

Once you recognize the need you are filling, consider finding another way to fill your need. Sonia sets aside 2 hours per week to spend with each child and enjoys it so much; she continues to be motivated by it. So faced with a bad habit you're trying to break, ask yourself:

+ What need or problem does this bad habit fill or solve?
+ How else can I solve this problem or fill this need?

Systems streamline a process or activity to improve your efficiency, but habits let you "set them and forget them." Once a habit is ingrained, it becomes very difficult to break but almost effortless to follow. When you create a habit of a certain behavior, it will actually be easier to do it than not to do it. This doesn't mean you won't work hard, but the hard work lies in establishing the habit in the first place.

SYSTEMS STREAMLINE A PROCESS BUT HABITS LET YOU "SET THEM AND FORGET THEM."

You must set goals to be successful. However, it is the habits you develop to help you achieve your goals that truly lead to success. If you set a goal to lose 20 lbs in the next two months, you're no closer to achieving it by setting the goal. However, develop a habit of taking the stairs instead of the elevator and you're already making progress.

If you want to take an exotic vacation next year, change your habit of buying a fancy coffee and cinnamon bun each morning. Deposit that $5 a day into a savings account. Small daily efforts soon amount to significant progress. If you want to be more effective with your time, develop a habit of carrying and using your agenda at all times. Develop the right habits and you will achieve amazing things.

HABITS REDUCE THE ENERGY YOU WASTE RE-MAKING DECISIONS

Each activity that moves you toward your goals results from a decision. Unless you've made it a habit, you must consciously decide to perform a task. Each decision drains your energy reserves slightly, and each has the potential to be a bad decision. For example, though you are trying to increase the amount you exercise, if, instead of creating a habit, you choose to decide each morning whether you will take the stairs or the elevator, you risk talking yourself out of taking the stairs "just this once." If the activities that move you toward your goals are not habits, you may even forget to do them altogether.

Create habits and you eliminate numerous decisions each day. This conserves the energy normally required to remember the actions you plan to take each day, and saves the energy you would need to motivate yourself to make the correct decision and perform the task each time. Habits use far less energy because you avoid the decision completely, you don't need to remember what you're supposed to do and there's no motivation required. Develop habits that move you toward your goals and you'll achieve your goals without even thinking about it!

WHAT SHOULD BECOME A HABIT?

Any repetitive activity you do frequently over a long period, such as exercising every day or taking your lunch to work, are ideal candidates to become habits. The habits you choose to hone must support your objectives. Some habits are "maintenance" habits; even if they don't directly contribute to achieve your objectives, they don't hinder your progress and they help you conserve energy to meet your goals. The habit of brushing your teeth several times per day is an example of a maintenance habit.

Some criteria you can use to determine which activities to develop into habits:

+ Activities you do frequently,
+ Activities you sustain over long periods,
+ Activities that support you in achieving your goals, and
+ Maintenance activities that help you conserve energy so you can work toward your goals.

BUILDING NEW HABITS

Habits come last in the FLASH framework, not because they aren't important, but because you'll have a much better idea of what habits to develop once you've set your new goals. Once you know where you want to go, it's a lot easier to pinpoint the habits that will help you get there. Make your habits specific enough that they don't require a decision. For example, to become more active, the habit "I'll take the stairs every morning instead of taking the elevator to the office" is far more powerful than a general strategy like, "I'll always choose the option that provides the most exercise."

When you're developing a new habit, create triggers to help

you remember to take the action you're targeting. Use alarms, ask friends to help, leave yourself notes and anything else that will remind you of the decision you've made. This will become less necessary once you've established the habit. You'll find yourself doing the new action more easily than not doing it.

Don't skimp on dream building even while creating new habits. Developing new habits is challenging. You already have many habits ingrained in your daily routine, some of which work against the new habit. For example, if you decide to go to the gym when you get home, but you have an established habit of turning on the TV as soon as you walk in the house, you're in trouble.

However, for a Creative Genius, no challenge is insurmountable. If the TV causes problems when you get home, develop a new habit. Unplug the TV in the evening before you go to bed. You'll actually save electricity by not having your TV in standby mode all day, and when you try to turn it on, it will serve as an excellent reminder that you've decided to work out after work instead of watching TV.

Sonia finds that running her contracting business places enormous demands on her time. She can expect clients to call her cell phone at any time of the day or night. She decides that instead of providing clients with her cell number, she will ask them to use her office number instead. For this to work, however, she has to create two new habits.

While Sonia normally checks her phone messages when she arrives at the office in the morning, she will now also forward her calls from her office phone to her cell phone. This way, she can leave the office at the drop of a hat, to visit job sites, suppliers or potential clients as required without fear of missing phone calls. However, if this strategy is to prevent interruptions from client calls in the evening, she also needs to develop the habit of removing call forwarding in the evening before she leaves the office.

Patrick has developed several habits, including always taking the stairs rather than the elevator or the escalator wherever he goes as a way to increase the amount of exercise he gets without taking time away from his painting.

John has developed a savings habit. He starts saving $25 a month using an automatic payroll deduction to deposit the money in a savings account each month. Within a few months, he discovers that even though he felt he couldn't afford the $25 per month out of his budget, he doesn't even miss it. He increases the savings by another $25 a month. By gradually adding to his savings, John is now able to put $200 a month away with hardly any effort.

The first component of the FLASH framework is to Find your Fuel. One of the first and best habits to develop is one of regularly reminding yourself of the payoff. You're developing habits to help you achieve your goals, and you're working toward the goals because they'll help you realize your dreams. Keep your dream, your reason for doing all this work, in front of you to maintain your resolve.

Here are other ways you can increase your motivation:

+ Create external calls to action Ask a friend to join you at the gym or to call to remind you of your commitment. If your goal is to take responsibility for your health, find a dentist who calls you when it's time for your next appointment.
+ Invest: Pay to join a regularly scheduled group or a class so peer pressure obligates you to attend and to avoid wasting money.
+ Keep the objective in mind: Keep reminders (pictures, a song, etc.) of what you are trying to achieve handy at all times.
+ Reward yourself: Give yourself a small reward after completing a task. If you swim for 20 minutes, spend five minutes in the whirlpool. (Don't let rewards interfere with your hard work. Pie is not a good reward for going to the gym!)

+ Commit to others: Tell your friends of your goal and ask for their support and encouragement.
+ Celebrate each success: Do a "dance of joy" each time you finish another task on your road to realizing your goals.

MAKE IT EASIER

Reaching goals demands that you break out of your comfort zone, and taking small steps initially will help build motivation. Your resistance to a change will be proportional to the size of the change. You will also improve your chances of success when you:

1. Start small and build on your successes: Putting $2 in a jar every time you forgo a coffee or snack is far easier than trying to sock away $300 a month. Anticipating next year's beach vacation easily beats your desire for a snack or a coffee, and experiencing success as you watch your jar fill up adds to your motivation.

2. Commit to a small step that leads to success: When Patrick began his swimming workouts, on the days he didn't feel like swimming, he'd commit to going to the pool and changing into his bathing suit. If he still didn't want to swim, then he permitted himself to leave. Of course, usually once he'd made it that far, he felt silly not to go swimming.

3. It's far easier to form a habit when you attach it to an established one. When I decided to write this book, I developed a new habit of writing for 60 minutes each morning. I attached this new habit to having breakfast, which I never skip. As a result, it became very easy for me to establish this habit.

4. Put success in your path: John works out every day and keeps his gym bag at the door, and as soon as he gets home, swaps out the dirty gym clothes, gets his stuff ready for the next day and puts his bag at the door again.

5. Don't allow loose ends to stop you: Develop a system for any complex

activity and work to perfect it. If you want to exercise in the morning, find a way to get up earlier, prepare your equipment ahead of time, create an exercise program, and so on.

6. Create obstacles to "not doing it": When trying to reduce your expenses, freeze your credit card in a block of ice you keep in your freezer. It's accessible in emergencies, but you'll think twice about ordering a pizza!

7. Put temptation out of your way. If you want to wake up earlier each morning but keep hitting the snooze button, set your alarm volume to maximum and put it across the room instead of next to the bed.

REACHING GOALS DEMANDS THAT YOU BREAK OUT OF YOUR COMFORT ZONE, BUT TAKING SMALL STEPS INITIALLY WILL HELP BUILD MOTIVATION.

LONG-TERM THINKING

Every repetition of an activity helps turn that activity into a habit, and the more repetition, the better. Each time you repeat an activity, you strengthen the habit, so:

+ Celebrate every repetition, because each one helps you reinforce a behavior that will ultimately lead you to success.

+ Don't beat yourself up when you slip. Past efforts are not lost, so if you do slip, simply use your Fuel to build your resolve and start again right away.

Progress may seem slow, but change is cumulative. Anthony Robbins, the famous self-help author and motivational speaker, explains that most people overestimate what they can accomplish in one year, yet they dramatically underestimate what they can accomplish in ten years. Activities that once took you out of your comfort zone will begin to feel familiar. Soon, your comfort zone will expand and you'll be the person you need to be to achieve your goals and live your dreams.

CONCLUSION

Habits reduce the energy you waste remaking the same decisions each day. Building habits requires you to create new circuits in your brain, which is why, like following a new route through deep woods, it is very difficult initially, but becomes easier as the path becomes worn. These new circuits become stronger with repetition until the worn path is the easiest way to proceed, so to ensure you keep up with your new habits while the path is being worn, create triggers that remind you of your new habits and your motivation for creating them.

Replacing a bad habit with a new, forward-moving habit requires that you identify the need that is being met by the old habit and developing new, more supportive ways to satisfy that same need. Will power wears out too quickly, and unmet needs will always drag you down and slow or stop your progress.

- ✦ Habits allow you to set systems and then forget them

- ✦ Habits eliminate remaking decisions, which can be difficult for Creative Geniuses

- ✦ When breaking a bad habit, replace it with a good habit

  - Consider what need the bad habit fills
  - Fill the need in a different way.

- ✦ When building a new habit,

  - Make the habit specific enough not to require decision-making
  - Create triggers to help you remember
  - Anchor them to existing habits
  - Make it automatic
  - Put success in your path
  - Develop systems to support your habits
  - Create obstacles to bad habits

- ✦ Celebrate every repetition

- ✦ Don't beat yourself up when you slip

PART TWO. REALIZE YOUR
DREAMS – CONCLUSION

Achieving your goals demands that you set SMART goals: specific, measurable, action-oriented, and realistic with a timeline. This allows you to set a course, evaluate the results and adjust your approach as needed. It also lets you know when you should celebrate! The FLASH framework allows you to achieve your goals. It stands for:

+ Find Your Fuel, the source of your motivation.
+ Use Layered Learning to learn through experience.
+ Achieve with Action combined with Layered Learning allows you to take effective action sooner.
+ Simplest Possible Systems reduce boredom, streamline actions and reduce the time you spend on routine or repetitive activities.
+ Hone your Habits lets you "set it and forget it," automatically achieving success by unconsciously repeating the right actions.

If you feel you'd like to get into action right now to build your dream, visit Succeed in a FLASH at **www.succeedinaflash.com.**

For additional information and support, visit Coach Linda Walker at **www.CoachLindaWalker.com.**

PART THREE

BUILD ON YOUR NATURAL RHYTHMS

CHAPTER 10
Tap Into Your Natural Rhythms

CHAPTER 11
Map Your Tasks

CHAPTER 12
Perform at Your Peak

PART THREE. BUILD ON YOUR NATURAL RHYTHMS – INTRODUCTION

Most personal productivity strategies, programs and systems treat organizing your time as a logistical problem. You have 168 hours in a week, 24 hours in each of the seven days, just like everyone else. So theoretically, you should be able to accomplish the same things as everyone else. These strategies point out that since you can't manage time, you need to manage how you use your time, to manage the actions you take each hour, each day. To be as successful as the people you admire, all you need to do is learn to use those hours as well as they do.

With the best intentions, you grab your agenda and plan out what you'll do each hour for the entire week. Or at least you try to make a plan. It's hard to estimate how long you'll need to get things done, and since you were tired Sunday night when you made your plan, you really didn't schedule past Wednesday. The next morning, you're facing one of those days. It's hard to get "in the mood." You try to tackle that project you've been dreading, but despite your best efforts, you make no headway. According to the carefully laid plans in your agenda, you should be on your third activity of the morning, but you still haven't made any headway on the first!

The next three chapters will help you optimize your natural energy cycles in a Creative Genius-friendly way.

CHAPTER TEN
||||||||||||||||||||||||||||

TAP INTO YOUR NATURAL RHYTHMS

Traditional approaches to improved productivity have a fatal flaw. As a Creative Genius, your productivity fluctuates dramatically with your energy levels. Hours are not interchangeable. Dedicate an hour of your time to writing a proposal when you arrive early at the office and you might zip right through it. However, if you were to take on that same task in the middle of the afternoon, you might struggle for two hours before giving up and promising to get back to it the next day. You cannot trade one hour for another. Depending on the natural rhythms of your energy fluctuations, if you don't have time to accomplish a task in the morning, you may be better off waiting until the next morning to complete it rather than attempting to continue it in the afternoon.

In this chapter, we'll introduce a new way of improving your productivity without working harder. You'll discover that by taking advantage of your natural energy fluctuations, you'll dramatically improve your effectiveness without increasing your net energy expenditure. In fact, you'll likely accomplish far more while spending less energy. You'll discover you have at least three very different energy states that vary over time, and as you learn to recognize these energy patterns and when they occur for you, you'll be able to optimize the way you work to take full advantage of them for daily tasks.

Sonia, our entrepreneur, struggles with a lack of structure caused by the demands of a growing business. Though she tries to plan how she would use her time in her agenda, Sonia can't stick with her plan. Emergencies take her off track and despite working late to catch up, she is severely behind in her work, feels overwhelmed and finds her life is out of balance.

Once Sonia realizes you can't compare hours to hours as you can "apples to apples," she is able to adjust her work schedule around her varying levels of energy throughout the day. Applying this knowledge allows her to get back on track with her plan.

In one dramatic example, instead of preparing a proposal, which requires long periods of concentration, in the afternoon when she feels her mental energy is typically lower, she reschedules it to the next morning. With that one scheduling change, Sonia is able to complete a proposal within 30 minutes, a task that normally took her two hours in the afternoon, and she felt it was of better quality than usual!

You accomplish tasks when you assign actions to time periods. Time is involved, but unless you perform actions, there is no productivity. If you want to improve your productivity, everyone has the same two choices, Creative Genius or not:

+ You can take more action in each hour, or
+ You can make each action more effective.

Productivity improvement demands more than fitting more activities into a given timeframe. To achieve maximum productivity, you must match an activity to a scheduled time, but you must also match the type of activity to your own energy level at that time. If you're unaware of your own energy fluctuations (they're not the same for everyone), and you're unaware of which type of activities work best with which energy levels, you're likely to schedule activities to match almost anything but your own energy patterns.

In fact, this is the approach most commonly recommended by many time management "experts." Obviously, it is important to honor your commitments, so traditional time management teaches you to schedule activities according to your commitments:

+ Do things when other people (spouse, boss, co-workers, kids) ask (tell) you to,
+ Work according to an imposed schedule (class times, store hours, appointments), and
+ Leave tasks to the last minute, scheduling around deadlines.

But that's exactly the wrong approach for a Creative Genius as it makes it very difficult to get things done. Arranging your schedule according to your own energy patterns lets you be so much more productive, it's the difference between climbing Mount Everest and strolling down a country lane.

ARRANGING YOUR SCHEDULE ACCORDING TO YOUR OWN ENERGY PATTERNS ALLOWS YOU TO BE SO MUCH MORE PRODUCTIVE, IT'S THE DIFFERENCE BETWEEN CLIMBING MOUNT EVEREST AND STROLLING DOWN A COUNTRY LANE.

SET YOUR OWN PRIORITIES

To fit in some quiet time to catch up on his work, John has been sticking around the office in the evening when everyone has left for the day. However, despite putting in the hours, he isn't making much progress. He doesn't seem to be able to get much out of his quiet time in the office, and he is extremely frustrated because the long hours are robbing him of time with his family with little to show for it.

Once he realizes that because of his personal energy fluctuations, the early evening is one of the worst times for him to do work that requires focused thinking, we are able to create a schedule that allows him the quiet time he needs when his energy is optimal for that type of activity. A few simple changes in his approach allow him to do the analytical work he needs to do and catch up easily.

RECOGNIZING YOUR ENERGY PATTERNS

Your energy fluctuates throughout your day, but to make things simple, we'll create three broad categories according to your mental and physical energy levels. They are

+ Focus Time, when your mental and physical energy levels are high,
+ Action Time when your mental energy is low but you still have physical energy, and
+ Recharge Time when you feel completely depleted.

FOCUS TIME

Most Creative Geniuses have periods of high mental energy when it's easier to tackle activities that require focus and concentration but they have other times when they struggle to focus even on tasks they normally find easy. You can recognize these fluctuations from changes in your ability to concentrate or to perform demanding mental activities. During periods of high mental energy, you easily achieve a state of hyperfocus, the state people often describe as "in the zone," when you participate in activities you find particularly interesting, especially activities that use your strengths. If you've never felt "in the zone" or experienced a state of hyperfocus, you may have yet to discover your true strengths or talents.

Learning to identify and take advantage of these high-energy periods gives you a secret productivity weapon. Match your

"Focus Time" with activities that require your concentration, pique your interest and play to your strengths; this is a recipe for hyperfocus. When in hyperfocus, you are able to concentrate at levels that exceed anything a neurotypical is usually capable of achieving. When you hyperfocus, you unleash the full power of your Creative Genius to accomplish amazing things.

MATCH YOUR "FOCUS TIME" WITH ACTIVITIES THAT REQUIRE YOUR CONCENTRATION, PIQUE YOUR INTEREST AND PLAY TO YOUR STRENGTHS; THIS IS A RECIPE FOR HYPERFOCUS.

Realizing that he has two Focus Time periods each day, Patrick begins to use his Focus Time in the evening to create his art. A talented artist, Patrick finds painting and drawing exhilarating and it definitely plays to his strengths. For Patrick, painting requires long periods of intense concentration working quietly in front of his canvas, so he learns it's best for him to paint during his Focus Time. Until he recognized that his energy levels follow a particular pattern, he would often set aside time to paint, only to discover he just "wasn't in the mood," and when he did create, his lack of enthusiasm left him feeling dissatisfied with the results. He didn't realize he simply didn't have the right mental energy to tackle that type of activity.

Now, he schedules time for painting during his Focus Time, when his energy is optimal, and he slips easily and predictably into a state of hyperfocus. Matching his activity with his energy levels maximizes his productivity and his creativity. He also finds this approach far more enjoyable than trying to paint when the energy isn't there, hoping inspiration will hit.

LEARN TO LISTEN TO YOUR BODY AND YOUR MIND, AND GO
WITH THE FLOW. YOU WILL UNLEASH A CREATIVE GENIUS
WHO WILL ASTOUND YOU!

Your energy level fluctuations are not quite as predictable as a train schedule, and events and circumstances can affect your normal patterns. If you're experiencing high stress or abnormal sleep patterns, you may be too tired to concentrate even during your usual Focus Time, and when inspiration hits, you may leap out of bed wakened from a sound sleep and achieve hyperfocus almost immediately. Learn to listen to your body and your mind, and go with the flow. You will unleash a Creative Genius who will astound you!

ACTION TIME

When your mind is over-active, jumping from idea to idea, you are likely fighting an urge to fidget, pace or take some sort of action. Your cognitive hyperactivity is compensating for your need to be moving. Years in school followed by work environments like a corporate "cubicle farm" have taught you to stifle your physical movement to avoid disturbing your neighbors. Unable to concentrate, you find this time unproductive and frustrating; you want to be up and moving. However, if you embrace, rather than fight, your natural tendency, this becomes the ideal time to get things done, at least if you choose the right things to do. John uses his action time to book his meetings, respond to emails and phone calls.

No, this is not the time to sit down and work on a mentally demanding task, but it IS the perfect opportunity to go to the dry cleaner or grocery store and to take care of various other errands. It's often an excellent opportunity to clean (though not necessarily to organize) your house or office. Physical activity such as yard work, home renovations or exercising at the gym, in the pool or outdoors is a far more rewarding and productive use of your time.

On the weekends, Patrick begins using his Action Time to cook for family and friends. He's able to keep everything under control in the kitchen, set the table in the dining room and participate in the conversation with his guests at the same time. He actually finds he's more comfortable participating in the conversation if he can be doing a physical activity at the same time. Cooking as he's chatting with his family or guests allows him to be more focused and less impulsive in the conversation and in his cooking.

Sonia learns to use her Action Time to do on-site visits, make phone calls or meet prospective customers. These tasks are usually short, require limited concentration and are more physical than the focus-demanding tasks of preparing proposals or writing marketing material. The interactivity of her exchanges with clients keeps her energy high.

John responds to emails and makes phone calls during his Action Time. He uses his Focus Time strictly for technical work like programming and writing.

Routines are extremely handy during these times. When your body just has to move, routine activities that you can do without thinking, or while your mind wanders, increase your productivity.

TIME TO RECHARGE

Some engines run hot. Creative Geniuses are like that. Capable of extraordinary productivity, especially when hyperfocused, you need time to recharge and let your high revving engine cool down. Overwhelm is a sure result of insufficient recharging time.

SOME ENGINES RUN HOT. CREATIVE GENIUSES ARE LIKE THAT.

111

We recognized the need to recharge in years past, and still to-day in some countries many people indulge in an afternoon siesta. A 20 to 30 minute nap allowed them to rejuvenate and be ready for the afternoon. In fact, this is so effective in improving productivity by making you sharper, more effective and less prone to error that it's coming back into vogue in some forward-thinking companies. Some companies have gone so far as to set aside quiet rooms where employees can take short naps or meditation breaks.

YOU NEED TIME TO RECHARGE AND LET YOUR HIGH REVVING ENGINE COOL DOWN.

Unfortunately, in most areas of the world, we have eliminated the siesta. Instead, we push through our fatigue, not realizing that doing so ensures we will not bounce back from our energy dip.

Use recharge time for any activity that replenishes your energy; for some people, it may be a nap, for others it's exercise. Reading, listening to music and meditation all allow you to slow down and siphon off excess stress. Taking a break to watch TV, play video games or surf the Web is tempting, and while these activities may allow you to relax at first, they are dangerous to anyone seeking to maximize productivity. These activities are so addictive that while you may intend to indulge for only a few minutes, before you realize it, many hours have passed. Studies also show that over time, they sap your energy rather than restoring it. You risk wasting high-energy Focus Time accomplishing little. For peak productivity, you must also use recharging time efficiently.

John had developed a habit that, though he felt drained, he'd push through his fatigue since he was not yet finished his work and he felt guilty for needing a break. In doing so, however, he accomplishes little or nothing. Too tired to concentrate, he becomes frustrated and wastes time ruminating. He now finds that if instead, he takes a break and goes for a brisk walk, he's rejuvenated and more productive when he returns to work.

Depending on your activities, you may need frequent breaks to reduce stress. Your "engine" (brain) runs hot. Running at full speed all the time is unwise. Running at full speed over rough terrain is worse. Your brain will overheat (and you'll feel overwhelmed). Treat your Recharge Time as sacred. Putting off a recharging "break" may provide you the illusion you're being productive, but you will pay dearly for it when you no longer have energy reserves to draw upon.

DEPENDING ON YOUR ACTIVITIES, YOU MAY NEED FREQUENT BREAKS TO REDUCE STRESS.

Occasionally, even though you had planned time to recharge, you may find you have plenty of energy. We all have good days and bad days. This is more likely to happen if you're working on something that piques your interest and plays to your strengths. When they start their business, entrepreneurs often find that MORE WORK on their business is a recharging activity! If that happens, use your recharging time for any activity that replenishes rather than drains your energy. Just, never infringe on your recharging time.

After painting on Saturday and Sunday mornings, Patrick fought his need to recharge in the afternoon. He couldn't imagine it would be more productive to take a break rather than to continue painting. However, he began taking 20-minute afternoon power naps to recharge. At first, he felt guilty, but soon he realized the increased productivity, the result of getting his second wind after his naps, more than make up for this down time. At work, he has no place to take a nap so instead he goes to the gym to exercise. He finds his energy improves greatly.

Learn to recognize when you're in Recharge Time. Unfortunately, you may not gradually lose energy or feel sleepy. Rather, the first sign you're tired will be an inability to concentrate and you may feel fidgety. You may lack emotional control. The surest sign you're not allowing sufficient time to recharge is an increasing feeling of anxiety or overwhelm. At Recharge time, you'll be more productive by taking a break to replenish your energy reserves.

CONCLUSION

In all cases, Focus Time, Action Time and Recharge Time, you'll increase your effectiveness and efficiency when you schedule the right task at the right time or select the right time for the right task. Select activities that require the most mental energy during Focus time. Choose short or physical tasks during Action time when you may not have as much mental energy but feel the need to move. Finally, do not force yourself to work through your Recharge time as it is counter-productive. You'll be far more effective taking a break to recharge your batteries and getting back to work with renewed vigor during your Focus time.

Now that you're familiar with the three types of energy patterns, we'll delve into the characteristics of tasks and the impact they might have on your energy levels.

✦ Optimize productivity by matching activities to the best time of the day for you to achieve it

✦ Focus time:

- Mental and physical energy are high
- Your brain is calm
- You can concentrate for long periods of time

✦ Action time:

- Low mental energy but relatively high physical energy
- You can only concentrate for short periods
- You feel like moving

✦ Recharge time:

- Your energy is completely depleted
- Use this period to replenish your energy levels

✦ Chart your energy patterns to first identify Focus and Recharge time

If you feel you'd like to get into action right now to build your dream, visit Grow With the Flow at **www.grow-with-the-flow.com.**

For additional information and support, visit Coach Linda Walker at **www.CoachLindaWalker.com.**

CHAPTER ELEVEN

MAP YOUR TASKS

Not all tasks are created equal. To improve task planning, look at each task and rate it for your interest around this task, the level of concentration the task requires, if it requires you to sit quietly for a long time or move from one component to another, and how long completing the task will take.

In this chapter, we'll see which task characteristics you must take into account when scheduling them for completion.

LEVEL OF INTEREST:

The interest you have in completing a task is important. Each person has his or her own level of interest in different tasks. While one person might find a particular task extremely interesting, another might find the same task bores them to tears. Your level of interest in a task is THE most important characteristic to determine how likely you are to complete it.

> YOUR LEVEL OF INTEREST IN A TASK IS THE MOST IMPORTANT CHARACTERISTIC TO DETERMINE HOW LIKELY YOU ARE TO COMPLETE IT.

Patrick is not, by nature, a "people person." Interactions with others leave him uninspired. He's quite impulsive and has a quirky sense of humor. He worries about saying something inappropriate, or blurting out something at the wrong time. He's often found that something he said unintentionally strained the conversation. However, he finds it easier to converse if he's able to be physically active at the same time. He's adapted his habits to take advantage of this discovery by incorporating walking into many of his interactions; he often conducts meetings while walking around the block.

Sonia, on the other hand, loves interacting with clients; it's one of her favorite aspects of the job. She's very outgoing and has a high level of interpersonal skills. John too enjoys working with people and is an excellent team builder.

CONCENTRATION:

Your ability to accomplish a task at any given time depends on the level of concentration required to complete the task and your ability to meet these requirements at that time. A task that requires a high level of concentration requires a significant investment of mental energy and necessitates sitting still for long periods. Reading difficult technical documents, writing essays or preparing proposals are some examples.

John manages the details of several projects to make sure they progress smoothly and that the needed resources are allocated and available at the right time. This work requires high levels of concentration as he works through long lists of tasks and juggles resources between two or three different projects simultaneously.

The intricacies of her numerous proposals requires a high level of mental energy for Sonia. When preparing proposals Sonia needs to break down each project so she can estimate how long it will take for her crew to complete each, the equipment and supplies required, the timing of work and how much each component will cost. Only then can she provide an estimate of start and delivery dates as well as pricing.

PHYSICAL ACTIVITY:

A physical task doesn't confine you. While these may not seem like physical tasks, John uses Action time to check his email, return phone calls and even arrange some meetings.

Physical tasks 1) put you in motion (cleaning your desk); 2) don't require long periods of sitting still and concentrating (phone calls); and 3) may be interactive or require jumping from one thing to another (responding to emails, conducting quick meetings and returning phone calls). Sonia is so at ease interacting with people that she is able to treat interacting with clients as a physical task.

For Patrick, who struggles to keep his mind from wandering when he interacts with others, or who struggles to pay attention to people who speak slowly, interaction is not a physical task as it demands a lot of mental energy. For him, physical tasks include walks around town scouting subjects for his next painting, sketching and taking pictures, cooking, exercising at the gym and swimming.

TIME REQUIRED OR LENGTH OF TASK

The Creative Genius brain often takes a bit of time to get up to speed, and demands even more time to transition between one activity and another. Creative Geniuses typically accomplish short tasks with very little effort most of the time. When you work on a long or complex task, manage the timing of that task carefully. How long does it take to complete each task? The threshold between short and long tasks is the time you can concentrate during a period of lower mental energy but high physical energy, that is, when you still have energy but can't concentrate much. For most people this threshold is usually 15 minutes or less, though some people are able to concentrate for up to 30 minutes, depending on the activity. It may be more or less for you. Regardless, if it takes less time than your threshold time, it's a short task.

THE CREATIVE GENIUS BRAIN OFTEN TAKES A BIT OF TIME
TO GET UP TO SPEED, AND DEMANDS EVEN MORE TIME TO
TRANSITION BETWEEN ONE ACTIVITY AND ANOTHER.

Patrick's threshold tends to be closer to 30 minutes. Responding to most emails takes Patrick 15 minutes, well within that threshold. Taking pictures for his paintings or preparing preliminary sketches before starting a painting usually falls within this time and so can be short tasks. Painting a picture, where setting up to paint can take 15 minutes or more, is not.

For John, 20 minutes is the maximum amount of time he can concentrate during Action Time. Any task that takes more than 20 minutes is considered a long task.

CONCLUSION

Realizing that each task is not created equal, taking into account the level of interest an activity holds for you, the level of concentration required, the physicality of the activity and the amount of time each task requires provides clues to optimize your natural patterns of energy fluctuation.

✦ Map your tasks by

- Level of interest – THE most important characteristics of a task for Creative Geniuses
- Required amount of concentration
- Physicality
- Time required to complete

If you feel you'd like to get into action right now to build your dream, visit Grow With the Flow at **www.Grow-With-the-Flow.com.**

For additional information and support, visit Coach Linda Walker at **www.CoachLindaWalker.com.**

CHAPTER TWELVE
||||||||||||||||||||||||||||||||||||||

PERFORM AT YOUR PEAK

I t is important to understanding how your energy patterns fluctuate and analyze the characteristics of a task to determine the
best time to complete each task. Not only can you shave hours off
the time required to complete them because you make more efficient use of your energy, but it also allows you to conserve energy
and eliminate frustrations.

In this chapter, we'll explore some great examples of how understanding both your natural energy patterns and planning tasks
accordingly can make a dramatic improvement in the ease with
which you complete these tasks, allowing you to optimize your
productivity and effectiveness.

This one strategy allows Sonia to dramatically reduce the time
she spends preparing proposals. Proposals, which Sonia finds demand high levels of concentration because of their complexity, take
long to complete. She realizes she must complete proposals during
her peak times. She's never lost another client because she failed
to deliver a proposal; she never delivers them late anymore. In fact,
she usually delivers proposals by the next day. She's still working
to improve her efficiency with proposals given the required concentration time; she's limited right now to only completing one
proposal per day. If she meets two or three clients a day, she'll
need to either cut the time it takes to prepare a proposal or reduce
the number of clients she meets. Otherwise, she risks delaying her
proposals over time and returning to previous bad habits.

During her Action time, which tends to be in the late afternoon until around 6 pm, she schedules her site visits and appointments with clients. She delays her lunch until 1 pm, which is when she finds she has very low energy. She usually takes a nap or exercises during her lunch break.

Patrick, realizing that his peak time starts very early in the morning, arranged with his boss to start earlier, against company policies, so that he can write his technical reports in the morning, exercise during lunch at his company's gym and manage emails, short calls and Web research in the afternoon when he's in his Action time.

As we mentioned earlier, discovering his energy patterns has allowed Patrick to paint in the evening, when he has a second period of Focus Time. Painting requires a lot of concentration and since preparation and cleaning up take almost 20 minutes, it wouldn't be practical to schedule an hour for painting. Luckily, he has a period of almost three hours of Focus Time so he can still paint for a little over two hours. This discovery has allowed him to start progressing toward his goal of becoming a full-time artist.

John, now that he recognizes his peak energy period, is working to improve his effectiveness during this time. Combating interruptions is an uphill battle but he is developing strategies to deal with these interruptions and other disturbances, as we'll see a little later. He recognizes that knowledge of his energy patterns has the potential to improve all areas of his life and is working hard to take full advantage of it. In the meantime, he has begun to schedule his meeting in the afternoons instead of at any time of the day.

CONCLUSION

When Creative Geniuses know their natural patterns of energy and take advantage of peak times to complete mentally challenging tasks, use their Action time to complete less taxing tasks and to respect their need to recharge, they not only optimize their productivity, but use less energy and keep frustration at bay.

‖‖‖‖‖‖‖‖‖‖‖‖‖‖‖‖‖‖‖‖

KEY POINTS

+ During Action time, perform activities that require little concentration, are physical, or if they require concentration, they require it for short amounts of time

+ During Focus time, perform long tasks that require a lot of concentration

+ Respect your Recharge time by taking a break and engaging in an activity that gives you energy

If you feel you'd like to get into action right now to build your dream, visit Grow With the Flow at **www.Grow-With-the-Flow.com.**

For additional information and support, visit Coach Linda Walker at **www.CoachLindaWalker.com.**

PART THREE. BUILD ON YOUR NATURAL RHYTHMS – CONCLUSION

The three principle strategies we've explored in this section will change your life for the better.

Based on client experience, strategically identifying your Focus time and planning your schedule around the periods when you are most effective so that you reserve that time for tasks that require the most mental energy has the potential to more than double your productivity.

Honor your need to rest and rejuvenate by choosing activities that refuel you during Recharge time so you regain your energy. You'll not only be far more productive when you do resume your tasks, you discover you have energy left at the end of the day to invest in the activities that are important to you.

Always consider the characteristics of an activity when choosing when to schedule it in your agenda will prevent you wasting time by struggling to complete a task that would be easily accomplished at another time.

PART FOUR
WEAPONS OF MASSIVE PRODUCTION

CHAPTER 13
Set Effective Boundaries

CHAPTER 14
Declutter Your Life

CHAPTER 15
Break Bad Habits Before They Break You

CHAPTER 16
Eradicate Time Traps

CHAPTER 17
Stop-Doing the Wrong Things

PART FOUR.
WEAPONS OF MASSIVE PRODUCTION

It's frustrating not to accomplish things you've set out to do. You start the day with renewed energy, ready to move your projects forward and to put a dent in your seemingly endless To-Do list. Then life happens.

COMMUNICATION ADVANCES

Communication advances that were supposed to improve our productivity have contributed to, even created, the problem. We're so "connected" it seems impossible to get any peace and quiet or time to think. Your computer announces you have emails and the phone rings constantly. Your smart phone won't even let you escape demands on your time as it ensures every phone call, email and text message reaches you wherever you are. Cubicle farms and open-door policies have given everyone permission to intrude on everyone else. Each interruption distracts you, ruining your concentration and forces you to deal with the always-urgent demands on your time. And as soon as you've dealt with those interruptions, something else pops up unexpectedly and demands your immediate attention.

COMMUNICATION ADVANCES THAT WERE SUPPOSED TO IMPROVE OUR PRODUCTIVITY HAVE CONTRIBUTED TO, EVEN CREATED, THE PROBLEM.

POOR ORGANIZATION

Poor organization also wastes time and creates frustration. Looking for misplaced things heightens frustration as you search for your keys but also negatively changes your mood for the day. Without time to think, it's impossible to strategize, prioritize or plan. As you struggle desperately to get something (anything!) done, you engage in busy work; however, busy is not always productive. You cringe at the thought of having to attend another ineffective meeting. Not only are they time wasters but you also leave each meeting with yet another list of To-Dos you can't possibly accomplish.

POOR HABITS

Don't imagine your struggle is everyone else's fault; at least some responsibility for your ineffectiveness lies squarely on your shoulders, and you're certainly the only one who's going to deal with the problem. Your poor habits are obstacles to productivity. Saying Yes too quickly puts additional projects on your plate, projects you really cannot afford to do. Rumination and daydreaming interrupt your work, and chances are your activity choices outside of work do nothing to improve the quality of your life. If you choose to watch TV, play video games, live vicariously through social media or surf the Web instead of engaging in exercise or activities that will provide you with a richer, more fulfilling life, are you not at least partly to blame?

> YOU DON'T NEED TO BE A VICTIM OF YOUR "CRAZY BUSY" LIFESTYLE.

You don't need to be a victim of your "crazy busy" lifestyle. You can avoid many of the sneaky hurdles your fast-paced, overbooked, driven lifestyle throws in your path as you work toward your objectives. Your struggle to do everything is actually preventing you from finishing what's most important.

In the next five chapters, you'll learn strategies for managing ever the ever-growing list of obstacles to productivity.

CHAPTER THIRTEEN
||||||||||||||||||||||||||||||||||||||||

SET EFFECTIVE BOUNDARIES

The global economy has opened many opportunities around the world, so companies must now serve clients 24/7. Client expectations have also grown, demanding fast service at their convenience, not only during your work hours. This also raises local customer service expectations. If your customers can get 24-hour service from across the continent or around the world, they don't understand why you can't offer the same thing. Cell phones have become a "staple" in our daily lives. There's no peace away from your desk, or out of the office. People can reach you anywhere.

In this chapter, we'll see how setting boundaries will enable you to take control of your productivity. Setting boundaries is simply an effective way to teach others how to treat you.

CALLS AND EMAILS

Sonia's clients' expectation that she be available 24/7 affects Sonia's life dramatically. Her phone never stops ringing. Clients call at all hours to check the status of their construction projects, or to ask questions. To make matters worse, Sonia always answers her phone when it rings. There is never any time to spend with her family or to eat in peace. Her family resents the constant interruptions of their conversations and activities with her. They also feel neglected, when Sonia leaves the room to speak to her clients as soon as her phone rings, sometimes in the middle of family discussion.

Sonia needs to establish boundaries if she is ever to reclaim her personal life. This means setting work and communication hours with her clients ahead of time, and communicating these clearly, even including them in the contract. She sets her office phone to reroute calls to her cell phone automatically during hours she's available and removes Call Forwarding on her business phone after hours, letting people leave messages at the office. She struggles with this, worried that her clients will get mad and go elsewhere. After working out an appropriate time for clients to contact her so that even clients who work during the day have ample time to call her with concerns, she resolves to try it.

She modifies her next contract and makes it a point to explain to clients when and how they can communicate with her. When she explains to them that she used to be available all the time and had no family life, they are sympathetic and are more careful of when they choose to call her. She also makes it a point to call her current clients on a weekly basis to make sure there are no concerns and that they are happy with how things are progressing. Her first try at this new schedule proves effective so she decides to change her contracts permanently. She manages client expectations from the beginning of their relationship; her clients feel well served, and both she and her family are very pleased with the results.

YOU TEACH OTHERS HOW TO TREAT YOU.

You teach others how to treat you. When you allow people to drop in or call you at any time of the day or night, you're teaching them that it's ok. If you teach them differently, they'll understand and are more likely to respect your time. If they don't, ask yourself "do I really want to work with someone who can't respect me?"

Instant communication channels, such as email, increase expectations as well. When you click Send, you know the recipient will receive the email nanoseconds later. Emails and cell phones have allowed us to do business after business hours. It also perpetuates the tendency to put out fires; we've become a nation of firefighters! We're constantly putting out fires because we don't take time to think of the next steps or proactively work to prevent problems.

John suffers from his own lack of "pro-activity" and that of his colleagues. He rises at 5 am every day to check emails his colleagues send overnight so he can answer them on the train ride to work. When he arrives at the office, his phone and email interrupt him constantly so he can't do his work. He stays at the office until 10 pm to finish his work, often at the last minute. If he misses the train and has to drive to work, he can't answer emails in the car. His colleagues get irate and wait at the entrance of his cubicle when he arrives because he hasn't answered their 5 am emails!

Yes, his colleagues have unreasonable expectations, but his past behavior has taught John's colleagues to expect this level of service. They have learned that they do not need to be proactive so every email is an emergency, another fire to extinguish.

After completing *The Maximum Productivity Makeover* program, he decides to limit his time for checking emails. From now on, he does a quick 15-minute verification of his emails in the morning after he gets to the office, and then answers them after lunch and again at the end of the day.

OPEN-DOOR POLICIES AND CUBICLE FARMS

In the '80s and '90s, companies instituted open-door policies as a way of seeming more "human." Everyone in the organization had to be at anyone's disposal. Managers who closed their doors were reminded, "We have an open-door policy!" Then as a way to cut costs by reducing floor space, businesses eliminated most closed offices and replaced them with cubicles.

Of course, it's impossible to close your door in a cubicle. Unfortunately, these cost-cutting measures allow neighbors to drop by at any time to talk to you about their latest "beef" with the boss or the TV show they saw last night. Employees talking to each other or on the phone also disturb their neighbors. If you have any difficulty concentrating, as John does because of his ADHD, you really struggle to stay focused.

Working with an "Interruption Log," a tool we use in *The Maximum Productivity Makeover* program, John tracks the source of his interruptions throughout the day. He notices a few patterns. One of his colleagues, Bill, disturbs him frequently about an important project they are working on together. John would stop everything to talk to Bill, even during his peak performance time. Unfortunately, he doesn't just lose the 10 or 15 minutes spent with Bill; he notices transitioning back to what he was doing takes as much as 20 minutes or longer, and sometimes he never gets back to it at all, instead moving on to a different project, leaving tasks incomplete.

John and I work on a process and script he could use with colleagues who disturb him during his Focus Time. When colleagues come to see him about non-work related issues, he usually asks to meet them at lunchtime. For colleagues such as Bill he establishes a 15-minute standing appointment in the afternoon during his Action Time. Bill stops interrupting John during his Focus Time because he knows they'll look over the project together during their meeting.

When he's working on a particularly difficult or important project, John posts a sign outside his cubicle, mentioning he's not to be disturbed and instructing people to either email or leave a voicemail if they need to meet with him. He prevents other people's lack of planning from interfering with his own plans.

Patrick, as a technical writer, also works in a cubicle, but his is in a high-traffic area next to the printer. There is a lot of noise from people chatting in the printing room as they wait for the printer to complete their request. He purchases noise-reducing headphones and listens to music as he works. People walking by also create a distraction for him so he moves his desk to face the wall. These measures improve his concentration dramatically; he's much more productive and rarely misses a deadline.

CONCLUSION

The need to communicate and stay connected, while important in today's business context, robs Creative Geniuses of focus and makes you less effective. Identifying your interrupters and using strategies to reduce them and creating and communicating boundaries allow you to stay focused and be more effective.

◆ Setting boundaries and communication

◆ You teach others how you treat them when you allow them to interrupt you

◆ Set specific times to check emails and answer phone calls around your energy patterns

◆ Communicate to others how you expect them to communicate with you

- Write it in your contracts
- Explain it verbally
- Modify your voicemail message
- Set standing appointments with those that require more communication with you

If you feel you'd like to get into action right now to build your dream, visit Cut the Crap: Eliminate Obstacles to Productivity at **www.JustCuttheCrap.com.**

For additional information and support, visit Coach Linda Walker at **www.CoachLindaWalker.com.**

CHAPTER FOURTEEN

||||||||||||||||||||||||||||||||||||||||||||

DECLUTTER YOUR LIFE

In this chapter, we'll cover strategies for decluttering your life. Decluttering is not just about our physical environment, although that is important and is addressed in this chapter. You also need to set aside time to think and plan, learn to manage your thoughts, focus on what's important and handle one of a Creative Geniuses biggest time wasters, meetings, effectively and efficiently.

With time to even think on back-order, there's very little time available to get organized. Implementing strategies to get organized enough that it doesn't interfere with our productivity can save a lot of time and energy.

NO TIME TO THINK – BUSY VS. PRODUCTIVE

Hard work is also making you less productive. Today we wear our "busy-ness" as a badge of honor, telling (bragging to) others how incredibly busy we are. This is supposed to prove you're really "going places," that you've earned your pay and that you're "promotion material." However, as we've noticed before, busy is not the same as productive.

Anytime anyone asks Sonia how she is doing, she always replies proudly how busy she is. To her, being busy is synonymous with being successful. Once she understands that her "busy-ness" might not be productive, she reexamines how she is doing things and realizes she is missing opportunities to streamline certain processes in her business, such as invoicing and proposals.

HARD WORK IS MAKING YOU LESS PRODUCTIVE.

When this becomes apparent to her, she decides to schedule three-hour appointments with herself every week to plan and design new systems to improve aspects of her business. Sonia finds it difficult to have three hours of uninterrupted planning time so she works offsite and turns off her cell phone during that time.

Choosing a labor-intensive approach over an automated, delegated or outsourced solution is another way we get busy without being productive. Sometimes a slower start would allow you the time to think of better ways to do things.

Sonia has been holding onto documents her bookkeeper needs to complete her already late income tax returns, stating that she seldom drives to that area. When I suggest she consider other ways to send the documents, she realizes she hadn't even searched for an easier alternative. She automatically reverted to the most labor-intensive solution as a habit to control spending. However, she soon realizes, you can always get more money, but you can never get lost or wasted time back.

INTERRUPTING YOURSELF

Your very active Creative Genius' brain can be a source of distraction as you encounter one brilliant idea after another. Each new idea takes your focus away from the previous idea so you make no progress implementing any of them. Unfortunately, your enthusiasm isn't just for your own ideas; your impulsivity makes you even busier when you get excited about a project someone else is describing and "accidently" volunteer for it!

After completing the Interruption Log, many of my clients discover that most interruptions come from their own thoughts. Lured by their brilliant ideas, Creative Geniuses often find themselves daydreaming, or jumping from one project to another, never focusing on one long enough to bring it to fruition. As a result, many feel frustrated and wonder if they'll ever achieve anything.

This is the case for John and Patrick. John's own thoughts often interrupt him. He has an idea and pursues it by researching it on the Internet. Unfortunately, it doesn't end there, as one idea leads to another and another, until at the end of the day he has chased a dozen different ideas but never implemented any. Improving his self-awareness around his peak performance time helps but there are times when he still pursues these searches.

FOCUS THREE

Besides improving his focus through better energy use, John needs extra help to keep his focus, well, focused. Many Creative Geniuses feel unproductive because they don't get through their very unrealistic daily To-Do List. However, most people only complete three significant tasks, that is, tasks that require an hour or two, each day.

Given John's propensity to deviate from his plan for the day, he makes it a habit at the end of each day to write the top three priorities for the next day that he has planned in his agenda on a colorful Post-It Note that he sticks to his monitor. The next day, he is reminded of his priorities before he even turns on his computer. Each time he deviates from his plan and takes notice, the Post-It Note interrupts his thoughts to refocus on his priorities.

In addition, when an idea really tempts him, he jots it in an "Idea Journal" for future reference when he actually has time to pursue these ideas. It calms his mind to have a place he can "park" his ideas. He doesn't feel he's denying himself the pleasure of learning something new, just delaying it.

WORKING OFF-SITE

When working on projects that require more concentration, request permission to work off-site. You may need to overcome initial distrust; your boss may worry that you won't work if she's not watching you. One of my former bosses was dead set against his employees working remotely because he assumed we wouldn't work if we weren't at the office. One day, because they were varnishing the office floors, the fumes were affecting my asthma and prevented me from staying in the office. I arranged to send my boss my finished work throughout the day. He was impressed with how much I accomplished when I wasn't subject to the usual interruptions and became much more flexible on other occasions when I asked to work from home. If your boss isn't very trusting, reassure him or her by sending regular updates of what you've accomplished.

MAKING MEETINGS MORE EFFICIENT

Disorganized meetings create stress. Every meeting takes more time than necessary, generates a lot more work for each person involved, and because you spend so much time in meetings, you have less time to do your work.

Poor meeting planning is a major source of productivity problems. Even if you rarely organize meetings or feel you have little or no control over how productive they are, there are many things you can suggest to improve meeting effectiveness. People almost universally regard meetings as a waste of time so they'll appreciate any suggestions that reduce their number and duration, wherever those suggestions come from!

As a project manager I had the opportunity to greatly improve meeting management and I've developed this section to help you reduce the negative impact they have on your productivity.

John is often called into meetings. He also chairs many team meetings each week. Everyone hated these meetings; the consensus is that they are a big waste of time.

John resists changing the way he manages his meetings. He feels people are used to a certain way of doing things and he doesn't want to rock the boat. I challenge him to set the example by improving how he manages his own meetings and he might get more support than he anticipates. He agrees to try.

First, each time he is tempted to call a meeting, he questions whether another communication method is more appropriate. He finds that for quick decision-making or idea generation meetings, email discussions are far more efficient than a face-to-face meeting. He sends an email explaining the problem he needs to resolve. He includes a request that people submit their ideas before a deadline (pick a time before you send the first email or you'll never hear from anyone again.) He gathers and lists people's proposed solutions and redistributes the assembled list to the group, and asks that each participant submit their vote for the top three by email. After compiling the votes, he announces the selected solution.

WHEN A MEETING IS INEVITABLE

Sometimes meetings are inevitable and are the best way to communicate as a team. For these occasions, John implements steps to make them as efficient as possible. Here are a few steps he implements:

1. He establishes the agenda ahead of time, pre-setting discussion time limits for each topic, and transmits it with his invitation to each participant. This allows everyone to prepare for the meeting and to have relevant information readily available.
2. He requests that each participant reporting to the group prepare and distribute a summary of the important information so attendees can read them ahead of time and prepare questions.
3. He ensures only people who need to be in the meeting are invited and he assigns clear roles for each attendee on the agenda.

4. He takes the minutes, produces and distributes them quickly after the meeting. He schedules preparing the minutes in his agenda immediately after the meeting while it is still fresh in his mind. His minutes went from being four or five pages long to a one- or two-page document containing only important information such as decisions and next action steps. This improves the completion of Next Action Steps as it reminds everyone of their assignments shortly after the meeting.

5. He eliminates irrelevant or off-topic discussions but, if the topic warrants discussion, it is added to the "Parking Lot" – a flip chart of questions and off-topic subjects to be discussed at the end of the meeting or in a future meeting.

6. Finally, John makes sure he schedules his meetings during his Action Time as he feels the interaction keeps him focused.

The new steps reduce John's meeting times by 50 to 70%. His team's projects begin to move forward more efficiently. Over time, his superiors and colleagues come to see him as an efficient meeting manager and he receives a lot of positive feedback about his meetings. In fact, many of his colleagues begin to emulate him so that even meetings he attends as a participant become more efficient.

Patrick's work also requires he meet with colleagues in other branches of the company. This was a very frustrating part of his job; he plays telephone tag with them to set up the meeting, and often when they do meet, he chases them again to get information they didn't have available at the meeting. To save time, Patrick schedules telephone meetings using his Outlook© calendar meeting request option, sending the questions ahead of time to help his colleagues prepare the information needed for his report.

GETTING ORGANIZED SAVES YOU TIME, ENERGY, MONEY AND MORE

There's a financial incentive for being organized. When you're organized, you don't incur late fees because you forgot to return your library books (or because you can't find them), you don't get speeding tickets because you're late for another appointment and you don't need to replace all those things you've lost!

IF YOU STRUGGLE WITH CLUTTER, YOU ALSO STRUGGLE WITH DISTRACTIONS.

If you struggle with clutter, you also struggle with distractions. A cluttered physical environment often signals a cluttered mind, but worse, it's very distracting. You also waste a lot of time searching for things and spend a lot of money replacing the things you never find.

John often forgets where he places important things such as keys, wallets, glasses and cell phones. Like the proverbial absent-minded professor, many Creative Geniuses don't pay attention to what they do with their things.

To solve this problem, John establishes a "drop-off area," a space near the door (at home and at the office) where he deposits everything he carries with him each day. He now only has one place to look for his keys, sunglasses, PDA, cell phone and bus pass that were easily visible. For his electronic equipment, he plugs in their rechargers near the "drop-off area."

Sonia's problem is two-fold: she loses track of her purse at the office and at home and; when she does find it, she can't find her things in it. She is forever emptying her purse to find her keys, her sunglasses, or her cell phone. Like John, Sonia uses a "drop-off area" when she is at work and another at home. She starts using purses and bags with more compartments and assigns a compartment each for her phone, her keys, and her iPhone. Not only does she save time and ease her frustration, she also feels more in control.

The common theme in these examples is that each thing needs a "home." I teach my clients to put new things they've acquired that don't have a home yet in a "Homeless Shelter." The Homeless Shelter is a clear plastic container you keep in a specific place where you store things that have yet to have a specific place to be. It's similar to a "junk drawer," except for one important aspect: it is only a temporary home. Once a week, you go through the Homeless Shelter playing social worker and decide on a home for each item. Make a habit of giving every item a home and returning items to their home each time and you will save you hours of searching.

CLEAR THE CLUTTER

Clutter distracts you. A desk piled with papers isn't conducive to work, and a cluttered home is not a place you can relax. You create clutter because you don't put things away after you use them, and clutter always gets worse because you purchase things you don't really need or you don't throw out the things you meant to replace with your purchase. Clutter also happens when you use things to fill an emotional void.

MANY PEOPLE USE THINGS TO FILL A VOID LEFT FROM NOT HAVING THE LIFE THEY WANT FOR THEMSELVES.

Why do you have clutter? Most clutter stems from a belief. You may believe that the things you own define you or that you won't be able to live without them. Many people use things to fill a void left from not having the life they want for themselves.

For others, it's a matter of disorganization and distraction. You forget where you put your keys because you were not paying attention when you put them down. You've bought your fifth pair of running shoes because you can't find the other four pairs you own.

Sonia discovers her clutter results from her numerous purchases made to ease the anxiety she feels from missing time with her family. With so little time left at the end of the day, she buys her kids things to relieve her guilt. These accumulate and create clutter.

Making time for her family and reducing work intrusions into her family time allows Sonia to eliminate that guilt and stop unnecessary purchases.

CONCLUSION

Many of the strategies discussed in this chapter apply equally at work, at home and in outside activities such as committees or volunteer organizations. Developing the habit of regularly taking time to think of how to improve processes, using strategies such as the Idea Journal to curb your tendency to interrupt your flow with chasing ideas, focusing on three priorities a day, and assigning a place for every object in your home and work area will reduce frustration and calm your mind. It also saves you time, energy and money.

||||||||||||||||||||||||||||||
KEY POINTS

+ Simplify your life

+ If you tend to interrupt yourself with bright ideas, keep an Ideas Journal handy to park them in

+ Focus on 3 tasks per day

+ Work off-site for projects that require more concentration

+ Make meetings more efficient

  - Establish an agenda ahead of time with preset discussion times
  - Require that each participant prepare and distribute a summary of important information
  - Invite only those who need to be there
  - Take minutes, produce and distribute them quickly after the meeting with only 1) decisions and 2) action steps
  - Park irrelevant discussions
  - Schedule meetings during the right time for you

+ Clutter costs you time, energy and money

  - Create a drop-off area next to the door for things you need when you're away
  - Clutter is distracting you
  - Take time to think of where new purchases will go – discard of things they are replacing and find them a home

If you feel you'd like to get into action right now to build your dream, visit Cut the Crap: Eliminate Obstacles to Productivity at **www.JustCuttheCrap.com.**

For additional information and support, visit Coach Linda Walker at **www.CoachLindaWalker.com.**

CHAPTER FIFTEEN

||||||||||||||||||||||||||||||||||||||||||

BREAK BAD HABITS
BEFORE THEY BREAK YOU

Creative Geniuses are not immune to poor habits. Over commitment, rumination and adrenaline addictions are all poor habits that can keep you from having a full and enjoyable life. In this chapter, you'll learn to recognize these and other bad habits that often keep Creative Geniuses from achieving their personal goals, and you'll also learn strategies that will allow you to break these bad habits with ease.

WHEN YOU SAY YES, YOU SAY NO

Sonia often finds herself overwhelmed because she volunteers for too many organizations. Networking had helped her build her business and she is heavily involved in several networking organizations, such as BNI (Business Network International), her local Chamber of Commerce, trade groups and charitable organizations. Each time she is invited to join or get involved in some project, not wanting to ruffle feathers, she says "Yes."

Sonia explains that she just can't say "No". However, as I explained, she does say No, in fact she says it too often. When she says "Yes" to one thing, she is saying "No" to something else. The "something else" she says "No" to include family time, time to think or even time for sleep. She needs to choose what she says "Yes" to more carefully.

She starts by identifying what is most important in her life considering her vision for her life in five years. Then when someone asks her to volunteer, she hesitates, but when she sees she has disappointed him or her, she relents and agrees after all. She needs to be better prepared to make the right choices, the choices that serve her best.

We work together to create a script for her to reply to requests to get involved. She memorizes it and even practices it in role-playing with me. The script is helpful to her, as now she can say "No" without feeling as if she is letting them down. Though she is tempted to say "Yes" at times because the project is so interesting and really speaks to her, she knows that she needs to consider what other projects she could drop before taking another one on. I usually recommend dropping two or even three projects you've been working on for a while before you say "Yes" to another because new projects usually demand more of your time in the beginning as you learn the ropes.

MANAGE YOUR MOOD

Your mood is also important. Ruminating, replaying a situation or event repeatedly in your mind, berating yourself or others for real or imagined mistakes or for not doing what you feel you should have done, will snowball a small issue into a big one. When you're in a bad mood, your negative thoughts preoccupy and distract you, so you must develop strategies to manage your mood, and break the cycle of rumination when you do fall into that trap.

THAT'S MY STORY

Most of our bad moods are created by the story we tell ourselves about what's really happened. As humans, we try to understand and find meaning in what is happening and associate events that are happening with the memories or thoughts these events trigger.

For John, his mood is his biggest obstacle to getting things done. Some small incident makes him lose his temper and his bad mood gets worse as the day continues. The strategy John and I devise is to 1) notice his bad mood when it starts; 2) engage in more effective self-talk. He asks himself, "What really happened?" "What story am I creating here?" "Is this productive?" then; 3) "What can I change about it right now?" and do it; 4) if there isn't anything he can change, he replaces the bad thought with an enjoyable or neutral thought. Notice that he does not attempt to stop thinking about it.

When you try to avoid a thought, you only think about it more. Instead, think of something else to distract you from the negative thought. To illustrate this strategy, if I ask you to avoid thinking of an elephant with a tutu, the image you form in your mind is that of an elephant with a tutu. If instead, I tell you to think of a penguin on a snowboard, you no longer think of the elephant.

BETTER COMMUNICATION

You can prevent many bad moods by improving your communication. Patrick is very sensitive to his wife's comments, often misinterpreting what she says. Deeply hurt, he blows up and stops talking to her. At times, he stews in his bad mood for days over something she's long forgotten. Patrick learns to assert himself in a more constructive manner.

Patrick really struggles with his emotions and attempts to talk to his wife about his feelings in the past have only ended in an explosive argument. Now he and his wife write letters to each other to communicate their feelings and their intent in order to improve the relationship. They decide on rules such as staying away from making accusations or hurtful comments. By writing letters, they each have time to choose their words carefully. Over time, they both realize they do not mean to attack or hurt each other and that often the problem is with their false assumptions.

Eventually they are able to communicate directly without writing everything down. Instead of losing his temper and assuming the worst, Patrick learns to breathe deeply to calm down or even to take a break from the conflict to collect his thoughts. Then he calmly and politely says what is on his mind in a non-accusatory way and asks for her point of view. Most of the time, he learns that his perceptions are wrong. And at other times, his wife has an opportunity to realize that things she says could be misinterpreted and to apologize.

NIP RUMINATION IN THE BUD

Rumination happens when you hang onto a negative thought. Everyone ruminates occasionally. Usually triggered by an event, rumination can create a huge black hole of productivity in your day, not to mention a malaise. John often becomes frustrated if other drivers cut him off. He loses his cool as he thinks about how terrible the world has become and how nobody respects him. "They're all out for themselves," he often repeats.

Arriving at work, he tells his colleagues how he's just avoided a collision and ruminates about it all day. Now in a bad mood, he notices every unintentional slight from his colleagues. This feeds his belief that nobody respects him and he becomes morose. He can't concentrate on anything else but this negative thought and as a result, doesn't feel satisfied with his day.

While working with me on *The Maximum Productivity Makeover* coaching program, John is able to nip rumination in the bud because he notices when it is beginning. He shifts his thoughts away from "everyone's out to get me" to a more empathetic "the poor guy probably got up late this morning and now he's running to make up for lost time; I know how that feels." Realizing the problem belongs to someone else helps John stop the rumination before it starts.

ADDICTIONS

ADRENALINE JUNKIES

Patrick is an adrenaline junkie whose worst habits include hours of television or playing video games, all while proclaiming he has no time for his art. Many people don't consider this a productivity issue because you're usually only wasting your own free time. However, a full and happy life includes making time for the things that make you feel fulfilled and alive. Many of the reasons you don't achieve your goals are linked to the choices you make about how you spend your free time.

THE REASONS YOU DON'T ACHIEVE YOUR GOALS ARE LINKED TO THE CHOICES YOU MAKE ABOUT HOW YOU SPEND YOUR FREE TIME.

For Patrick, the problem is that he only scheduled work-related tasks and activities he needs to complete in his agenda. You've heard the old adage: "Those who fail to plan, plan to fail." By not planning how to use his free time on evenings and weekends, Patrick fills his time with whatever activities are easy to access. To paint, he needs to plan ahead because pulling out his paints and setting up takes a bit of time. As he doesn't plan, he ends up opting to watch TV, wasting hours on social media or playing video games, which wastes his time and his talent.

This is not to say you should never watch TV, keep up with your friends on social media or play video games. These activities can be quite entertaining; however, their abuse makes you less productive. Instead of watching show after show or playing endless video games, select the shows you want to watch or how much time you will spend playing video games, schedule them in your agenda and then stick to your plan. Limit yourself

153

to the shows or playtime you schedule and fill the rest of your time with activities that allow you to develop your talents and strengths, develop more and better relationships or to explore new interests.

When Patrick begins to schedule time for his art, he honors these commitments to himself. He begins to enjoy his life more and soon increases the number of hours he devotes to his art.

MEDIA JUNKIES

Sonia's bad habit is her addiction to information. She collects information, clipping articles that might interest her friends or that she might want to look at later, but this is taxing her time and cluttering her desk. Sonia subscribes to two daily newspapers and many more newsletters by email, not because they are relevant to her, but because they are nice to know. She rarely has time to read them but keeps them in her inbox just in case, although she does read her newspapers; she feels she has to be current on the news so she can converse with clients.

Many Creative Geniuses are addicted to information. Insatiably curious, they subscribe to numerous RSS feeds, electronic newsletters, magazines and newspapers, constantly wanting to know more, and they stockpile reference material "just in case". Absorbing, storing and managing all this information consume time and energy, thus becoming an obstacle to productivity.

I ask Sonia how she would handle a conversation with a client if she didn't already know all the details of current events. She realizes she could easily ask questions to learn whatever she doesn't know. She finds people enjoy impressing her with their knowledge, and when she asks them questions and lets them do most of the talking, they find she is a brilliant conversationalist.

Sonia cancels one newspaper and unsubscribes from all newsletters that are not immediately relevant. This frees time for strategic thinking in the mornings, which allows her to write in her journal and ponder the direction she wants to take with her business.

CONCLUSION

Creating free time in your life will enable you to pursue personal goals. Avoid over commitment by learning to say "No" graciously. A script you've prepared ahead of time prevents you from saying "Yes" to someone else when you don't feel you have time to say, "Yes" to your own desires.

Take control of any addictions to TV, social media, Internet, video games and information so you can schedule better, more enriching activities in your free time. And should you slip up, stop rumination in its tracks by first noticing when it starts, questioning your thoughts immediately and choosing to think differently.

✦ Say "Yes" to yourself before you say "Yes" to others

✦ Stop rumination before it takes over your day by

- Considering what really happened
- Recognizing the story you created from it
- Using neutral thoughts to explain

✦ To achieve your goals, make choices in how you spend your time, commit to yourself

- Say "No" to TV, video games, and say "Yes" to your projects

If you feel you'd like to get into action right now to build your dream, visit Cut the Crap: Eliminate Obstacles to Productivity at **www.JustCuttheCrap.com.**

For additional information and support, visit Coach Linda Walker at **www.CoachLindaWalker.com.**

ERADICATE TIME TRAPS

The "time traps" we've been exposing in Chapters 13, 14, and 15 consume your time without your permission. We've covered some of the most common time traps, but you have your own unique challenges to deal with as well. To break your time traps, you need to decide how you will handle each one instead. In this chapter, we're going to discover the secret weapon to eradicate time traps, the Not-To-Do list.

Your Not-To-Do list evolves as you identify activities or people that use your time without advancing you toward your goals. This list describes the time traps you want to eliminate, and provides alternative actions to help you reach your goals. It is an essential tool in your "You Management" arsenal.

For example, one of John's Time Traps is constantly checking his email. He adds the following to his Not-To-Do List:

+ I do not constantly check my emails throughout the day; <u>instead</u>, I check email for 15 minutes at 11:30 am and again at 4:00 pm.

Patrick wants to stop watching unscheduled TV or playing video games. He adds these items to his Not-To-Do List:

+ I do not watch TV aimlessly; <u>instead</u>, I select no more than seven shows each week that I schedule into my agenda.
+ I do not allow poor planning to rob me of my time; <u>instead</u>, I will schedule two extra evenings a week for painting.

Sonia's Time Traps include taking phone calls during Focus Time and after work hours so among her many Not-To-Dos, she lists the following:

- ✦ I do not answer the phone during Focus Time; <u>instead</u>, I let calls go to my voicemail and return them when it fits my schedule.
- ✦ I do not answer work-related phone calls outside of work hours; <u>instead</u>, I remove Call Forwarding from my business line at the end of each day and allow my voice mail to pick up my messages.
- ✦ I do not say "Yes" on a whim; <u>instead</u>, I ask the person for time to think about whether or not I can commit to more. If pressed for an answer, my response must be "I'll get back to you on that" or "If I can't have time to check my schedule then the answer is "No".
- ✦ I do not book an appointment in my agenda without also scheduling sufficient time for travel and preparation.

WHAT TO DO WITH YOUR NOT-TO-DO LIST

Your Not-To-Do list is a work in progress. As you notice Time Traps, write them down and decide how you will handle them. Add those to your Not-To-Do list as required. As your habits change, you may wish to eliminate older items from your Not-To-Do list simply because they are no longer a problem.

Schedule time to read your Not-To-Do list in your agenda each day and every time you plan your time. Keep it in your agenda, and if you are using an electronic agenda such as Outlook, create a recurring task to pop up your Not-To-Do list for you to review every morning.

THE NOT-TO-DO LIST DOCUMENTS YOUR TIME TRAPS AND HOW YOU PLAN TO MANAGE THEM NOW AND IN THE FUTURE SO THAT THEY DO NOT CREATE OBSTACLES FOR YOU.

CONCLUSION

The Not-To-Do list documents your time traps and how you plan to manage them now and in the future so that they do not create obstacles for you. Reading them every day and each time you plan your week allows you to keep them fresh and stops you from reverting back to old habits.

✦ Create a Not-To-Do list

- List time traps
- Include how you will manage each
- Review each day and every time you plan your time

If you feel you'd like to get into action right now to build your dream, visit Cut the Crap: Eliminate Obstacles to Productivity at **www.JustCuttheCrap.com.**

For additional information and support, visit Coach Linda Walker at **www.CoachLindaWalker.com.**

CHAPTER SEVENTEEN

||||||||||||||||||||||||||||||||||||||||||

STOP DOING THE WRONG THING

A Not-To-Do list is useful to break habits that are making you less productive. However, you may be in a situation that demands more than just a decision to change. You may be doing things that do not play to your strengths just because there is no one else who can do them right now, either because you cannot afford their services or because you don't know anyone with the skills to do them. You may have taken on a job or a role that no longer serves you but changing the situation involves a big decision that affects other people, and requires planning and time to implement. In fact, for you to stop doing this thing is a project in itself.

This is not really a Not-To-Do list item, so in this chapter, we're going to learn how to create and use a new tool. This type of situation warrants an entry on your Stop-Doing list.

When John's aging mother fell ill, he took care of her every need. His two siblings never had time to help, or didn't feel they needed to because he had already taken over. However, between frequent appointments for his mom, work and taking care of his kids, he is disorganized, frustrated and exhausted.

Perhaps you've taken on a role you're not comfortable with, but that others expect you to play. Patrick always felt one of his roles as the "man of the house" is "fixing" things around the house. However, he does not enjoy anything about home repairs and he is admittedly not very good at it. He often has dozens of projects abandoned around the house because he is stuck, not knowing what to do next.

CONSIDER THE COST OF DOING IT YOURSELF

Consider whether you're actually getting the benefits you anticipated. Patrick isn't happy with the outcome of his home renovation projects and he soon realizes that his wife isn't impressed with the results either. He certainly isn't saving money when he has to call an expert to repair his handiwork. What benefit is he getting and at what cost? The mess created by his unfinished projects, his and his wife's frustration, and the time it takes to complete a project because of his inexperience, are clear signs that he isn't reaping any benefits from doing things himself. If you think the alternative is too expensive, think again! The same reasoning applies at work.

When I challenge Sonia to get a bookkeeper, she hesitates, thinking, "Why would I hire someone to do something I can do myself?" However, Sonia procrastinates doing her accounting for weeks. She hates it and has to psyche herself up to complete it. It takes her almost 20 hours each month to get her papers together and complete her accounting. Given her goal to reach $1,200,000 in sales this year, we estimate her time is worth $600 per hour. The opportunity cost of doing her accounting is $12,000 per month (20 hours X $600/hour). The cost of having it done by a bookkeeper: is 10 hours@ $30/hour or $300. It takes the bookkeeper less time because he is used to doing bookkeeping, enjoys it and has a system in place to streamline it.

In the meantime, Sonia can spend those 20 hours getting new sales, making new contacts or advancing a project more quickly. She can also spend the time relaxing spending quality time with her kids. She also saves the uncounted hours she used to spend worrying about her accounting without actually doing it. Having an unpleasant task to do is very distracting. The longer you put it off, the more it weighs on your mind. There's no formula for calculating this cost, but it is high. If you had the choice between paying $12,000 or $300 to buy the exact same thing (actually the lower priced product is of better quality), which price would you prefer? Why choose the higher price?

Momentum is extremely powerful, and can be helpful or harmful. Momentum is one of the best strategies for overcoming procrastination, but momentum also leads you to continue doing things the way you've always done them just because that's the way you've always done them. For John, momentum is making him responsible for his mother's care when he has two siblings who could help.

MOMENTUM IS EXTREMELY POWERFUL, AND CAN BE HELPFUL OR HARMFUL.

Often, you can resolve many challenges that disrupt your life if you simply stop doing the things presenting those challenges. Yes, there are things you must do, and it's true that you won't enjoy some of them. But you're probably doing many things you could stop doing, but that you continue to do because it's become a habit. Like Sonia, you may even be doing things someone else would be better suited to do because you think the alternative is too expensive but you'd be wrong! Use your Stop-Doing list to eliminate those activities that are preventing you from moving toward your goals.

For each thing on your Stop-Doing list doing, ask yourself:

+ Can I drop it altogether? Perhaps it's time to let go.
+ Can I delegate it? Perhaps a system could streamline it.
+ Can I pay someone else to do it? Ideally, I will use someone who's better qualified than me.
+ Can I barter with someone who's doing something they hate but I'd enjoy (or at least hate less)?

Patrick realizes he has to stop attempting his own renovations. He adds the following to his Stop-Doing list

✦ I no longer do my own renovations; <u>instead</u>, I find a good contractor I trust and whom I can call when needed.

Once Sonia understands she is losing money by doing her own bookkeeping, she adds this item to her Stop-Doing list:

✦ I do not do my own bookkeeping; <u>instead</u>, I hire an experienced bookkeeper and use my time to increase sales.

Sonia works on the items in her Stop-Doing List as if they were active projects, so she reviews her list every time she does her weekly planning. She soon finds an excellent bookkeeper and begins to delegate all her bookkeeping, along with several other items of paperwork he can handle better than she can. Fueled by how smoothly things are going and noticing that her business is flourishing with the extra sales and her own extra energy, she decides to add the following:

✦ I no longer prepare my own contracts or invoices; <u>instead</u>, I hire an experienced Virtual Assistant and delegate this work.

For John, asking for help is difficult because he doesn't want to neglect his mother. Nonetheless, he decides to trust his brothers to help care for her and adds this to his Stop-Doing list:

✦ I do not take it upon myself to be mother's sole caregiver; <u>instead</u>, I ask my brothers for help so that we share the responsibilities.

John also realizes that his brothers are eager to help but worried they won't be as good as John is at taking care of her. Sharing this responsibility with his brothers has added benefits; his mother has the opportunity to see all her children regularly and she enjoys that immensely.

WHAT TO DO WHEN YOU DECIDE TO STOP DOING

Once you know what you want to stop doing, what can you do about it? When you feel you're doing something you shouldn't, consider dropping it, delegating it to someone else or to a system, or delaying it until you have more time. Remember to let others know your plans and what's in it for them so you avoid facing resistance from others and instead, gain their buy-in. For more information on how to prepare others for changes you want to make, consult Chapter 21 on Getting Everyone on Board.

WHEN YOU FEEL YOU'RE DOING SOMETHING YOU SHOULDN'T, CONSIDER DROPPING IT, DELEGATING IT TO SOMEONE ELSE OR TO A SYSTEM, OR DELAYING IT UNTIL YOU HAVE MORE TIME.

Review your Stop-Doing list regularly allows to keep it top of mind so you can notice the opportunities that come your way.

CONCLUSION

When you struggle to do things that don't play to your strengths, you've taken on a role you're not comfortable with, or you continue to do something simply because you can and you're used to it, it's time to create your Stop-Doing list.

The cost of doing things yourself is huge: it robs you of your productive time, saps your energy and may even cost you money. Consider your Stop-Doing list as a project you work on actively to eliminate all but the best uses of your time, energy and Creative Genius.

✦ Create a Stop-Doing list that includes

- Activities that don't play to your strengths, talents, passions
- Activities that no longer serve you but that require planning and time to implement
- What needs to be in place to stop it? A system, delegation or bartering?

✦ Consider the cost of doing it yourself vs. if you :

- Drop it
- Delegate it to systems or others
- Delay it

If you feel you'd like to get into action right now to build your dream, visit Cut the Crap: Eliminate Obstacles to Productivity at **www.JustCuttheCrap.com.**

For additional information and support, visit Coach Linda Walker at **www.CoachLindaWalker.com.**

PART FOUR. WEAPONS OF MASSIVE PRODUCTION – CONCLUSION

Massive productivity improvement occurs when you take control of your life. To take control, you must set boundaries, letting others know how you want them to treat you. It also requires that you choose what's important to you and to eliminate the obstacles to achieving a life centered on your strengths, passions, interests and desires. It's also important to indentify your time traps and create a plan for overcoming them. Finally, drop or delegate all activities that don't meet your new criteria for what's important in your life.

If you're ready to let loose with your weapons of mass production but would like some help, visit www.JustCuttheCrap.com.

For additional information and support, visit Coach Linda Walker at **www.CoachLindaWalker.com.**

PART FIVE
TAKE CHARGE

CHAPTER 18
Select the Proper Tools

CHAPTER 19
Plan For Success

PART FIVE. TAKE CHARGE

IS THIS TIME MANAGEMENT?

The term, Time Management, is inaccurate. You cannot manage time: you can't stockpile it for later use, nor can you save it for a rainy day, borrow it or exchange it. You can't slow it down or accelerate it. The only thing you can really control is you. That's why I prefer the term "self-management", that is, managing "you" within your allotted 24 hours each day.

SELF-MANAGEMENT REQUIRES A 100% SOLUTION.

You cannot take charge of your life piecemeal. That's like steering a car only some of the time. The times you're out of control leave you so far off track, there's no way to recover. No one tool can provide a complete solution, but by selecting from the assorted tools you'll learn about in chapter 18, you'll assemble a solution that will work for you.

You'll learn about self-management strategies that allow you to achieve your goals, do what you need to do and still have time and, better still, energy left over to develop your strengths, interests and passions, to be the person you want to be and to feel empowered to take the reins of your life.

Many Creative Geniuses resist any form of control, even self-control. You don't want anyone to control you. You even resist establishing your own rules and structure as a way to control your own life. You fear that trying to control your life will stifle spontaneity and creativity.

This explains why so many Creative Geniuses don't use or carry an agenda. It might also explain why your life is out of control. If you forget commitments, tend to be late (if you remember the appointment in the first place), allow obstacles to get in the way of managing your life and never have time to do the things you really want to do or always feel you're playing catch-up, consider the benefits of taking control of your life.

The next two chapters describe the tools you need to manage projects and priorities in your life and provide you with a foolproof process for planning. You can adjust it to meet your needs, but we recommend you try it "as is" before attempting to modify it.

CHAPTER EIGHTEEN
||||||||||||||||||||||||||||||||||||||||||||||

SELECT THE PROPER TOOLS

As mentioned earlier you can't manage time; it is not under your control. However, you can manage what you do and how much you accomplish by choosing the best thing to do at the best time for you to do it. This chapter provides you with the tools to help you make the best choices so that you make progress toward your goals using a foolproof system for managing your life.

John resists the idea of structure, organization and self-management. A typical adult with ADHD, he doesn't even own a watch. He feels that so much structure does not leave room for spontaneity; he feels imprisoned. When he finally agrees to try imposing his own structure, he realizes how freeing it is to be in control. He realizes that when he wasn't efficient, he spent his "free time" scrambling to catch up.

When his wife asked for a divorce, he finally realized his ADHD was creating problems for her and his family. He often missed family events and broke his commitments to them. While the chances of reconciliation with his wife were dismal, he decided his relationship with his sons was worth protecting.

Sonia tries desperately to better control how she uses her time. As an entrepreneur, she understands that time is as valuable, if not more than money, so she keeps three calendars: a business calendar, a family calendar and her personal calendar. She constantly juggles activities between them. It's no surprised they frequently slip through the cracks.

A SYSTEM THAT WORKS LIKE CREATIVE GENIUSES DO

Creative Geniuses are visionaries, Big Picture thinkers, so your system must reflect this. You think in conceptual terms, that is, you like to see all the elements together instead of in bits and pieces. Creative Geniuses generally don't enjoy delving into details, especially about tasks that don't particularly interest you, so your self-management system must be high-level, simple and to the point.

Unlike many artists, Patrick has tried several time management systems, including Franklin Planners©, Day Timer© systems and other generic systems to get a handle on his life. He knows his wife is frustrated at being responsible for most household and family tasks. She takes care of the menu, grocery shopping, meal preparation, budgeting, cleaning, doing the laundry, plus she takes care of arranging for baby sitters, transportation to and from school and to activities, along with many other responsibilities required to take care of the kids. Oh, and she also works full time.

Unfortunately, all of Patrick's systems are bulky and too complicated. Because it's inconvenient, he rarely carries his agenda with him and so he often misses things that arise when he is away from his desk. He misses deadlines, forgets important tasks and arrives late (or not at all) for important meetings. After his most recent demotion, he realizes he needs help to create a system that will work for him.

A complete self-management system includes a strategy for adapting your activities to your energy patterns, a way to ensure and track progress toward your goals by creating systems and habits, strategies and tactics to overcome procrastination and tools to eliminate obstacles to productivity. And to make the best use of this system, you must know where you can have the biggest impact in the world.

A COMPLETE SELF-MANAGEMENT SYSTEM INCLUDES A
STRATEGY FOR ADAPTING YOUR ACTIVITIES TO YOUR ENERGY
PATTERNS, A WAY TO ENSURE AND TRACK PROGRESS
TOWARD YOUR GOALS BY CREATING SYSTEMS AND HABITS,
STRATEGIES AND TACTICS TO OVERCOME PROCRASTINATION
AND TOOLS TO ELIMINATE OBSTACLES TO PRODUCTIVITY.

From a logistical point of view, you'll require the following tools:

+ An agenda ·
+ Project Task lists
+ A To-Do list
+ A Not-To-Do list
+ A Stop-Doing list
+ A Routine Task List
+ A Personal Development List or Strengths and Interests List
+ Interactive alarms

Once you include all these elements in an integrated system, you'll have a 100% solution. Nothing will escape your notice or slip through the cracks.

Let's see how you can combine these elements to **take charge**!

CALENDAR OR AGENDA

Many Creative Geniuses don't have an agenda, and those who do usually use it only to manage appointments or meetings. It's rare to find a Creative Genius using an agenda to its full advantage.

John's only agenda is the one his employer imposes on him, the company has a standard electronic agenda used to schedule internal meetings based on participants' availability. Since John doesn't use his agenda other than to indicate when he has meetings, he always seems to be available so his colleagues book him at any time. He never uses the agenda outside the office.

Your agenda will be the hub of your Self-Management System. It is here you record all your appointments and routines, and here you record your plan for how you'll use your time each day. Your agenda supplements your memory and maps out the best times to complete your work, to schedule your commitments to family and friends and, most importantly, to block out your commitments to yourself, time you allocate to work toward your objectives.

I recommend a portable computerized agenda, also known as a PDA (Portable Digital Assistant) that synchronizes with your Calendar system (*Outlook©*, *Lotus Notes©* or other). Smart phones often offer this functionality as well. Portability ensures you can carry it with you at all times, and auditory alerts remind you of your commitments. However, you can design a paper-based system with the essential characteristics as well.

Your agenda serves several purposes. You'll use it to:

+ Capture appointments in real-time: As you make commitments or appointments with other people, you enter them immediately in your agenda (No more appointment cards to lose!). This ensures that you are available for the new appointment so you eliminate overbooking; and that your appointment is where you will look and find it – not on a piece of paper you'll end up losing on the way to the car.
+ Complete weekly planning: Unless you plan how you'll use your time, be assured someone (everyone!) else will. Your weekly planning is where you make commitments. Not only will you record your commitments with others, you'll also include your commitments to yourself.
+ Control your productivity: You'll consult it throughout your day to determine your commitments.

You'll use your agenda constantly so it must fit easily into your life, and to serve all these purposes well, it must have certain characteristics, as we'll see in the following sections.

A SINGLE AGENDA FOR YOUR WHOLE LIFE

It's essential that you have one and only one agenda to record relevant information about all aspects of your life, and remember, there's far more to your life than just your career. You have commitments to your family and friends, you have routines to track, appointments, related to work or not, that you must keep, and of course, work-related or other commitments.

Sonia with her three calendars quickly realizes her system is far from foolproof. On numerous occasions, she books client meetings in her work agenda that conflict with family and personal commitments. She often misses her medical and dental appointments, which are recorded in her personal agenda. It isn't difficult to convince her to move to a single agenda.

PORTABLE

To get the most benefit from your agenda, you must carry it with you at all times, and you must use it. Anything less than a 100% solution is no solution at all. You need an agenda small enough to be transported everywhere but large enough to be of use. If necessary, consider purchasing a carrying case that attaches to your belt or your purse, a shoulder bag, backpack or anything else you need to ensure your agenda is always with you.

TO GET THE MOST BENEFIT FROM YOUR AGENDA, YOU MUST CARRY IT WITH YOU AT ALL TIMES, AND YOU MUST USE IT.

John decides he doesn't like a paper agenda because his writing's too small and a PDA (Personal Data Assistant) doesn't allow him enough space to enter information. Instead, he opts to carry a PDA along with notepad to record new appointments after having checked whether in his PDA that he is free for the appointment. When he gets back to the office he enters the new appointments directly into his computer agenda and synchronizes it with the PDA.

A WEEK-AT-A-GLANCE

As a big picture thinker, your planning process works best when done on a weekly basis. To plan effectively each week, your agenda must show a week-at-a-glance with all seven days visible together, either in an electronic calendar, like *Outlook©*, *Lotus Notes©* or iCal or on opposing pages in a paper-based agenda.

TO PLAN EFFECTIVELY EACH WEEK, YOUR AGENDA MUST SHOW A WEEK-AT-A-GLANCE WITH ALL SEVEN DAYS VISIBLE TOGETHER.

It's very difficult to plan your time using a one- or two-day-per-page view because you'll need to flip from page to page to decide when you'll schedule a task. This taxes your working memory unnecessarily, leading to frequent mistakes.

The month-per-page view of smaller agendas doesn't provide enough space to write details of your activities, leaving you to rely on a notoriously unreliable memory. Planning your time fully will clutter your agenda making it difficult to read. The best system is one that works the way your brain is more comfortable.

Convinced, Patrick moves to *Outlook©* and purchases a PDA. As I suggest, he adjusts the view in his electronic calendar to show seven days in seven columns on the screen. He plans his activities on his computer, because when he synchronizes with his handheld device, he is only able to see one day of his agenda at a time on the small screen, but having the PDA allows him to have his schedule and audible reminders of tasks and appointments with him at all times.

COLUMNAR AGENDA

Many Creative Geniuses are visual learners. You'll find it far easier to manage your agenda when you can see your week at once with all seven days arranged in side-by-side columns. You are less likely to make mistakes this way and the columns provide visual cues to the time of day when assignments or appointments will take place. Sonia, who opts for a paper system, purchases a medium sized agenda with a week-at-a-glance view with the week spread across seven columns, one for each day.

SPACE FOR EVERY WAKING HOUR

Since your system helps you control your whole life, even in a paper-based system, you'll need space to record information for every waking hour of your day, and for every day of the week, not just for work hours. Miniature agendas will not do. An 8½ by 5½ inch size is ideal for a paper-based agenda as it shows you a week-at-a-glance and is convenient to carry with you. Ideally, you'll also have space for your To-Do list, but if that's not possible, we'll look at satisfactory alternatives a little later.

PROJECT TASK LIST

Life is a series of projects. Getting your kids back to school in September, making a meal and doing laundry are all projects. As soon as more than a single step is necessary to achieve a desired result, it's a project.

LIFE IS A SERIES OF PROJECTS.

Making meals requires you to 1) select recipes; 2) make a menu; 3) list the ingredients to buy; 4) shop for food; 5) put the food away; and then 6) prepare each dish following the appropriate recipe (each of which is a project in itself!).

For repetitive projects,, such as making meals, doing your laundry or cleaning the house, you developed a project plan, applied it, tweaked it and eventually created a system. You probably did all this without even realizing that's what you were doing, and because you practice it so often, you may not even keep a written project plan.

However, when you tackle new projects such as building a deck, writing a report, preparing a contract, purchasing a computer or home insurance, or creating a new presentation, you must prepare a Project Task list so you don't forget any steps.

WHAT IS A PROJECT TASK LIST?

A Project Task list is simply the To-Do list to complete one specific project. You create a separate Project Task list for each of your projects so you can keep your main To-Do list under control. Sonia keeps every task for every project she is involved in on her main To-Do list, and soon has a To-Do book! Her long To-Do list overwhelms her. In addition, when she has a cancellation and wants to take advantage of her free time to complete a To-Do, she finds that she has trouble selecting anything because her list is so long.

In each Project Task list, list the To-Dos for that project (at least the ones you know about now... you can add To-Dos to the Project Task list as you go along, so not knowing every step in a project is no reason not to get started!) that you plan to accomplish in the next week or so.

John resists the use of the Project Task List until he realizes that it keeps his To-Do list manageable and allows him to prioritize and plan his projects more thoroughly. When planning his schedule for the coming week, he doesn't need to sift through tasks due six months in the future. Those tasks are on the appropriate Project Task list until he needs to transfer them to the To-Do list.

CREATING A PROJECT TASK LIST

When developing your project task lists you do not need to develop the whole project plan in one sitting. That could prove overwhelming, time consuming and confusing. This is the case for John who works on long-term technology projects. In large projects, it might even delay the start of the project. Instead, he develops a list of milestones, points at which he can check progress because a sub-project or task has been completed, within his main project.

When Patrick and his wife decide to buy their next home, they develop a list of milestones that looks like this:

1. Purchase a new home
2. Give notices to break lease in current apartment
3. Send change of address notices
4. Pack boxes that can be packed ahead of time
5. Organize moving day
6. Complete last-minute tasks
7. Move
8. Unpack and enjoy! ☺

Each of these milestones indicates the completion of a sub-project, each of which is a project in itself and might even have sub-projects within it. Here's how the sub-project leading to the first milestone of "Purchase a new home," breaks down:
   a) Determine budget
   b) Create a list of criteria for ideal home

c) Select possible neighborhoods
d) Look at listings of homes for sale that fit criteria in newspaper and on the Internet
e) Select a home (a sub-project in itself)
f) Contact agents for appointment to view houses
g) Visit homes
h) Make an offer
i) Get home inspected
j) Apply for mortgage
k) Etc.

DEVELOPING THE PROJECT

Developing a list of tasks or activities for a project isn't rocket science (unless your project is to launch a rocket!). Some people list sub-projects first and develop each one in more detail separately. Others brainstorm and write down every task they can think of in no specific order.

Some people work backwards. They imagine their project already finished and then work backward through each task they did to reach that point. For example, they imagine they have already signed a lease for the new apartment. They ask themselves, what did I have to do just before signing a lease? I had to select an apartment (that goes on the list), and to do this, I had to visit several apartments (put that on the list too), and so on. They continue working back through the project until they get to, "Prepare project task list."

When developing a Project Task list, you will find you only need to do a few tasks in a specific order. You can do most tasks in any order, and you can even do some in parallel. You might decide to choose homes in the newspaper and online first and then make appointments before visiting the neighborhoods. There's no wrong order unless one task is dependent on the outcome of another.

ORGANIZING MULTIPLE PROJECT TASK LISTS

We are all involved in many projects at any given time, some large and some small. Sonia always has several active project related to her business.

She prefers a paper-based system to manage her project task lists and agenda, so we create a system in which she uses different colored pocket folders, one for each project. She attaches a Project Task list sheet to the front of each folder and writes the name of the project at the top of the list. She develops the project milestones that require special or customized resources first as she often needs to order these ahead of time. She adds additional milestones and tasks as the project advances and as she thinks of or discovers what the next steps will be.

She keeps any document related to the project, such as signed contracts, supply lists, invoices and team hours inside each folder and transports the folders in an attaché case.

Patrick prefers to use *Outlook©* Notes for his Project Task lists. He creates a note using the project name and adds each task or sub-project in the note.

In *Outlook©*, you could also use a Category name for your project name and then list your sub-projects as notes within that category. However, it may be difficult to keep sub-projects and tasks in order, and some PDA's limit the number of categories they will track or synchronize.

THE TO-DO LIST

Use your To-Do list to track the tasks, the due dates and the amount of time you estimate you'll require to complete them. This can be a "dangerous" part of your system because of these common errors:

✦ You confuse projects and tasks.
✦ You have a **To-Do book** instead of a **To-Do list**.
✦ You under-estimate the time required.

YOU CONFUSE PROJECTS AND TASKS

John's procrastination on one particular item in his To-Do list is creating chaos in his home life. When I ask him what it is, he says, "renovating the kitchen." Right away I see he is confusing projects and tasks. When I point this out to John, he immediately realizes why he's been stuck.

A few key questions have him developing the Project Task list for Renovating the Kitchen. As soon as he sees he needs to break his Kitchen Renovation project down into tasks, he is relieved and able to follow through. The following week he reports that he has already taken some significant action steps in this project.

YOU HAVE A TO-DO BOOK INSTEAD OF A TO-DO LIST

If your To-Do list is very long, it will be difficult to organize or prioritize, making planning a long, complicated process (which you'll avoid, thus making the situation worse), and it'll diminish the importance of each task. When your To-Do list is too long, you lose hope of ever making progress, which leads to procrastination.

KEEP YOUR TO-DO LIST AS SHORT AS POSSIBLE.

Keep your To-Do list as short as possible; a maximum of 5 or 7 items is best. To do this, use Project Task lists to record tasks for your various projects and use your To-Do list only to record tasks from each project that are due in the next week and tasks that are not part of a project. You may also find it useful to create categories for your To-Dos.

The way you categorize your activities depends on your situation. Some people prefer to categorize according to priority levels: A = very important/urgent, B = important, C = nice to do. Remember, however, that categorizing by level of priority, though commonly the default way of categorizing in many time management approaches, will not necessarily serve you well. Creative Geniuses have a "passionate mind." Your brain activates by interest or passion, not importance.

CREATIVE GENIUSES HAVE A "PASSIONATE MIND".

You may also categorize by context. As described by David Allen in *Getting Things Done*, you should categorize your tasks in terms of the situation you must be in to complete a task. Sonia categorizes her list of To-Dos for when she is in her car, for when she is in her office and for when she is at home. Tasks in the "context" of her car included errands, appointments or visits to friends or relatives. The only limit to the ways you can categorize your To-Do list is your imagination.

As an entrepreneur working mostly from home, I don't find categorizing by context particularly helpful. I group tasks by type of activity; I list phone calls together but separate from computer tasks, and so on.

Another client categorizes her to-do list by the type of energy required to complete it.

ESTIMATING THE TIME REQUIRED

You'll only complete tasks once you schedule them in your agenda, but to do that, you must estimate how long it will take to complete each task. Estimating time to complete a task can be very difficult for Creative Geniuses. For you, time is very fluid.

YOU'LL ONLY COMPLETE TASKS ONCE YOU SCHEDULE THEM IN YOUR AGENDA.

Adults with ADHD like John really struggle with estimating time. John forgets that he needs to allocate time for transitions out of the previous task, i.e. putting away things he used for the previous task he was working on, and shifting his attention away from it. Then he must transition into a new task: getting in context, remembering the status of the task, preparing the needed resources and shifting his attention to the new task. Transitions can take as long as 30 minutes, so it's important to account for them.

I suggest my clients avoid transitions, especially during their peak time, because 30 minutes lost during that period of the day represents a huge loss in productivity. Just scheduling work on tasks in longer "chunks" during Focus Time and saving shorter tasks for Action Time can double the work you accomplish in the same number of hours!

For John, I suggest he triple the time he estimates for tasks he doesn't do often. Many Creative Geniuses use this rule of thumb to compensate for their overly enthusiastic and optimistic estimates of the time required for a given task. He reports that the triple estimate is often closer to the mark than his original estimate.

For Sonia, her estimation fails to allocate time for travel. As a result, she usually drives fast from one client appointment to another and often receives speeding tickets. I encourage her to schedule travel time to and from her client appointments directly in her appointment book and she's never looked back.

Some activities require preparation. When Patrick first joins a gym and decides to attend first thing in the morning, he forgets that he needs time to prepare his gym bag, to travel to the gym, change into his gym clothes, exercise, take a shower and do his grooming, repack his bag and travel to work. He is often late for work.

To correct this pattern, he schedules the preparation of his gym bag the evening before as soon as he gets home and leaves earlier in the morning to make up for travel, shower and grooming time. Finally, he has to adjust his bedtime to get at least seven hours of sleep.

THE NOT-TO-DO LIST

Your Not-To-Do list addresses your personal time traps. Review your Not-To-Do list each time you plan your day or week and before booking anything in your agenda. Use it to filter out time traps before they occur. We discussed the Not-To-Do list in Chapter 16, How to Create a Not-To-Do List.

> YOUR NOT-TO-DO LIST ADDRESSES YOUR PERSONAL TIME TRAPS.

Sonia, who opts for a paper-based agenda, tapes her Not-To-Do list inside the cover of her agenda and reviews it regularly.

Patrick and John create recurring tasks so that their Not-To-Do lists pops up on their computer screens every morning for review.

THE STOP-DOING LIST

Your Stop-Doing list captures tasks that aren't really yours to do, but that somehow you've taken on.

> YOUR STOP-DOING LIST CAPTURES TASKS THAT AREN'T REALLY YOURS TO DO, BUT THAT SOMEHOW YOU'VE TAKEN ON.

While you may not yet be in a position to implement every item on your Stop-Doing list, review your Stop-Doing list during your Weekly Planning session and watch for opportunities to:

+ Delegate items from your Stop-Doing list to systems or to others.
+ Hire experts to take over items from your Stop-Doing list.
+ Barter items from your Stop-Doing list with others who would rather do your tasks than some of their own tasks that you'd enjoy doing more.
+ Drop activities you're only doing out of habit.

By reviewing her Stop-Doing list on a weekly basis, Sonia is open to new opportunities and soon meets a virtual assistant (VA) at one of her networking groups. After a short interview with her, she decides to hire her to prepare her invoicing and format her proposals, contracts and any other administrative work she could fit in the 10 hours per month she's contracted. The 10 hours her VA works saves Sonia over 20 hours of productive time because her VA is more efficient than Sonia at those types of tasks.

A couple of months after Sonia hires her VA, her sales begin to increase steadily as Sonia uses the 20-plus hours she has gained to make more contacts, pursue leads and close more sales. For more information on the Stop-Doing List, refer to Chapter 17.

ROUTINE TASK LIST

The Routine Task List contains details about routines you have integrated or wish to integrate in your day-to-day life. Setting a time for when you will complete each routine reduces decision-making and allows you to create other routines to support them. For example, to incorporate going to the gym in the morning, you'll need to establish a routine of preparing your gym bag the day before.

Some of my clients have morning, afternoon and evening routines as separate checklists for their different commitments. For example, Sonia's afternoon routine includes:

+ Pick up daughter at school

- ✦ Prepare gym bag for the next day
- ✦ Take food out of the freezer for supper
- ✦ Do homework with daughter

STRENGTHS AND INTERESTS OR PERSONAL DEVELOPMENT LIST

This is a list of activities you do regularly to develop a strength or interest, or a list of the activities you'll do as soon as you can "make space" in your schedule.

Sonia, who dreams of one day speaking to young women's groups, includes getting involved in Toastmasters to improve her public speaking skills on this list. Patrick not only includes painting classes but also networking with other artists on his Personal Development list.

John asks each of his sons to suggest activities they'd like to do together with him. Both are interested in martial arts so he enrolls them.

ADDITIONAL CRITERIA OF AN EFFECTIVE SELF-MANAGEMENT SYSTEM

AN INTEGRATED SYSTEM

Your self-management system must be fully integrated so it packages every component you need together. Depending on the type of work you do, you may need an additional notebook you carry with your agenda. As a project manager, there were so many tasks to track, with new ones popping up each day, that I incorporated a notebook into my system. I used it to take notes during meetings, and to capture reminders and additional tasks "on the fly," that is, when I wasn't as my desk.

NO MORE FLOATERS

Everything in your system – agenda, lists, contact information, notebook (if needed) – must be contained in one package, so that when you leave one place to go to another, you can grab it and go, assured you've left nothing behind. Both John and Patrick use their electronic agendas exclusively as their self-management system. Sonia adopts a hardcover notebook since she often needs to take notes on her clients' elaborate projects.

EVERYTHING IN YOUR SYSTEM – AGENDA, LISTS, CONTACT INFORMATION AND NOTEBOOK (IF NEEDED) – MUST BE CONTAINED IN ONE PACKAGE, SO THAT WHEN YOU LEAVE ONE PLACE TO GO TO ANOTHER, YOU CAN GRAB IT AND GO.

PORTABILITY

You will use your self-management system to track every part of your life, so you must carry it everywhere and anywhere you go. Invest extra, if necessary, to make your system conveniently portable.

Sonia carries her agenda and notebook together in a shoulder bag. Patrick specifically purchased a PDA that would also play music to encourage him to take his PDA everywhere with him. When he travels on the bus or subway, he's always listening to music on his headphones, so he never forgets his PDA.

INTERACTIVE SYSTEM

Finally, your system must include a way to remind you when you're supposed to do something. If you're using an electronic agenda, you can easily set alarms that will pop up on your computer and ring on your PDA. If you are using a paper-based agenda, you'll need to be more creative.

YOUR SYSTEM MUST INCLUDE A WAY TO REMIND YOU WHEN YOU'RE SUPPOSED TO DO SOMETHING.

With a paper-based system, Sonia used her cell phone and small electronic timers to keep her on track. Even though her cell phone didn't have full PDA functionality she is able to set it to ring alerts for appointments.

Sonia also develops the habit of checking her agenda before and after completing any task to ensure she sticks to her plan. This habit also ensures she relies less on alerts for everything since, over time, she tends to become desensitized to them. No matter how you organize your system, include integrated alerts that will keep you on track.

CONCLUSION

Having all the tools you need to build a foolproof system is an absolute necessity for Creative Geniuses. You require a portable system that includes a full week-at-a-glance agenda, a project task list for each project, a To-Do list, a Not-To-Do list and a Stop-Doing list. It must also include one or several routine task list(s) and a Personal Development list.

Your system must be fully integrated, portable and interactive to support your ambitious dreams.

The next chapter delves into how to use your self-management tools.

KEY POINTS

- ✦ Your planning system must be a 100% solution, leaving nothing to chance

- ✦ A complete self-management system includes:

  - A strategy for adapting your activities to your energy patterns
  - A way to ensure and track progress toward your goals
  - Strategies to overcome procrastination
  - Tools that eliminate obstacles

- ✦ Your agenda must:

  - Be portable – you'll need to take it everywhere
  - Be unique – a single agenda for your whole life
  - Show a full week-at-a-glance for planning
  - Have a columnar view of the week
  - Space for every hour

- ✦ Use Project Task lists to avoid having an endless To-Do list

  - Use Layered Learning to develop the project

- ✦ Your To-Do list must

  - Be a short weekly list
  - Estimate time required for each task

- ✦ Develop and review Not-To-Do list and Stop-Doing list regularly

- ✦ Have a Routine Task list for recurrent activities

- ✦ Devise a Strengths and Interests or Personal Development List

- ✦ An Integrated system should

  - Not have floaters, post-its and appointment cards…
  - Have everything in one system
  - Be portable
  - Be interactive with alerts to remembering

If you feel you'd like to get into action right now to build your dream, visit Master Self-Control at **www.TimetobeCreative. com.**

For additional information and support, visit Coach Linda Walker at **www.CoachLindaWalker.com.**

CHAPTER NINTEEN
||||||||||||||||||||||||||||||||||||||||

PLAN FOR SUCCESS

If you don't plan how you use your time, others will. Your agenda filled with your time commitments acts as a shield, keeping other people from filling your time with things they want you to do. Since time is your most valuable asset, it is essential you develop the habit of planning how to use it; even more important than planning how you'll spend your money.

In this chapter, you'll learn how to complete annual and quarterly planning, how to plan each week and how to manage your agenda to reach your goals.

Your planning process includes an annual and quarterly review of your vision, projects and goals to ensure you're still moving forward as you continue to strive to realize your vision. You also need to track each of your projects on a monthly or more frequent basis, since projects tend to change or veer off track. Weekly, you'll review your To-Do list and complete your planning for the coming week. Make adjustments daily or mid-week to move tasks you intended to complete at a certain time but didn't.

Your agenda will adjust to your changing life. It should. When an airplane leaves Los Angeles to fly to Hawaii, it is only directly on course for Hawaii about 6% of the time. It is constantly drifting off course, and the pilot must bring it back each time. However, in the end, the plane always lands at the targeted airport, and that's what's important.

Let's examine the planning process for each interval in detail.

ON A QUARTERLY OR ANNUAL BASIS
TAKE STOCK

Annually, it pays to take stock of your successes in the past year. John always feels he is never accomplishing anything. He forgets (or even dismisses as unimportant!) his successes and accomplishments, instead dwelling on what remains to do. Taking stock allows him to celebrate and to remember his achievements, which boosts his self-esteem.

Taking stock also allows you to reinforce what you've learned about yourself and the best approach for you. You have likely discovered previously unknown strengths, talents and interests, and you may have a better understanding of your values. The more you know about yourself, the better you'll be at choosing and managing projects to maximize your best qualities and overcome your biggest hurdles by assigning weaker areas to others.

THE MORE YOU KNOW ABOUT YOURSELF, THE BETTER YOU'LL BE AT CHOOSING AND MANAGING PROJECTS TO MAXIMIZE YOUR BEST QUALITIES AND OVERCOME YOUR BIGGEST HURDLES BY ASSIGNING WEAKER AREAS TO OTHERS.

As you take note of what you've accomplished, ask yourself:

+ What did I learn about myself?
+ What strengths did I use to accomplish this?
+ Are there any newfound strengths, talents or interests that became evident for me here?
+ Who (or what kind of person) did I become as a result of accomplishing this?

Keep an inventory of these new discoveries and accumulate your findings from year to year. You'll become increasingly aware and appreciative of just how special you are.

CELEBRATE YOUR YEAR AND WHO YOU ARE

Once you take stock, take time to relive your most amazing accomplishments. How did it feel? What kind of person did these things allow you to be? What are you capable of and what else does that mean you can accomplish?

PREPARE FOR THE COMING YEAR

Review your vision. Has it changed? When your vision is clear, you can identify projects and goals that will move you closer to realizing your vision in the coming year.

Consider where you want to be in a year from now in all aspects of your life. Where do you want to be in your career, in your personal relationships and in your financial situation? What do you want your health to be like? Where do you want to live? And to provide clarity as to your real purpose, ask yourself, "Why is this important for me?"

Now, compare where you want to be with where you are right now. What gaps lie between where you are and where you want to be? What projects, routines, habits and systems will help you close the gap?

Write down your goals for each of the areas of your life and review them at least quarterly.

MONTHLY PLANNING

Once each month (more often for critical or active projects) review your projects. Are they still on track? Have you completed the activities you had planned? Do you need to make adjustments?

Rarely do projects go exactly as planned or expected. Various factors, many of them out of your control, change the course of your projects. This is why you must review each ongoing project regularly, update your action plans and possibly revise your goals for the project.

WEEKLY PLANNING

Weekly planning (with an optional mid-week review) allows you to more easily consider events, commitments and deadlines coming up in the near future, and to gain a "big-picture view" of your week. As Big Picture thinkers, Creative Geniuses control their planning better on a weekly rather than daily basis. Once you try it, you'll probably stick with weekly planning.

Weekly planning saves time and takes advantage of how your brain works.

WEEKLY PLANNING SAVES TIME AND TAKES ADVANTAGE OF HOW YOUR BRAIN WORKS.

Here are the steps to manage your weekly planning:

1. Review and manage your projects to determine upcoming tasks.
2. Update your To-Do list with tasks from your projects, assignments and other tasks you wish to do.
3. Filter your To-Do list using your Not-To-Do list and your Stop-Doing list.
   a) Schedule activities in your agenda while accounting for deadlines, the time required for each task and your energy levels (see *Chapters 10 to 12* for more details on scheduling tasks based on your energy levels.)

Let's look at each step in more detail.

MANAGE YOUR PROJECTS

Review each active project and determine the next steps you'll work on over the next week or so. As you review your projects, add any new tasks that come to mind for each project to each Project Task list.

When Sonia reviews each of her active projects, she determines the next steps for each one. She has four renovation projects in progress and two new proposals to prepare for projects that could start in as little as two weeks from now. Each project and each proposal has its own Project Task List.

For one of her current projects, Sonia must follow up with an electrical contractor she needs on Wednesday of the coming week to add a new circuit. She must also check the status of supplies she ordered for delivery on Thursday. She writes these two items on the appropriate Project Task list. She further develops the To-Do lists for the other three current projects in the same manner.

UPDATE YOUR TO-DO LIST

Transfer each task of your Project Task lists to your To-Do list as its due date nears. Remember, only move tasks you'll be actively working on in the next week or two.

Sonia then transfers each task from her Project Task Lists to her To-Do List. She already has some personal tasks and other tasks not related to a project on her To-Do List. She has to make an appointment to see her dentist; she hasn't seen the dentist in two years because she always forgets to make the appointment. She also has to go shopping with her daughter for boots. Her husband has also asked her to proofread one of his university papers.

FILTER YOUR TO-DO LIST

As you can see, without systems for removing tasks from your list, your To-Do list will just get longer as you assign different things from your personal, professional and home life.

CHECK YOUR NOT-TO-DO LIST

What things on your To-Do list shouldn't be there? What will you do about them? Sonia filters her To-Do list using her Not-To-Do list. One item she notices on her agenda is an appointment she has made with a client for 1 pm on Tuesday; however, she realizes she has not booked sufficient time for travel to and from the appointment, one of her Not-To-Do's, so she corrects this. One of her Not-To-Do items is accepting project changes without documenting them with a sign-off by the client. She must also prepare a Change Request Form for a client so she schedules this on Tuesday morning.

John uses the same process; he notices a meeting invitation for one morning during the coming week. On his Not-To-Do list, he has noted that he doesn't book meetings during his Focus Times, which is in the morning. He schedules time in his agenda to contact the meeting organizer to negotiate a different time for the meeting.

John also must prepare a monthly status report compiling team members' reports on the project for noon on Friday. In the past, this meant he spent Friday mornings chasing reports from colleagues. In his Not-To-Do list, he has decided to check emails at the end of the morning and twice in the afternoon. He adds a To-Do to contact his colleagues to ask for their status report on or before Thursday at 5 pm. This allows him to clear Friday mornings to write the report instead of chasing his colleagues and constantly checking for their incoming emails.

CONSIDER YOUR STRENGTHS AND WEAKNESSES

Are there activities you've committed to do that don't play to your strengths? If there were tasks you planned to do but never did, are you procrastinating? If you've procrastinated, why is that? Do you lack interest in the task or is this a weakness for you? Can you inject interest or, better still, delegate it?

One of the tasks Sonia didn't complete the previous week is creating a proposal template. She can't delegate it, but it's not an interesting task so she decides she will complete it at her favorite coffee shop as a way to inject novelty into the mix.

Are there tasks/activities you have committed yourself to do to develop your strengths or interests?

HONOR PAST COMMITMENTS

Honoring commitments is important to ensure you build your credibility with people around you as well as with yourself. If you've committed to an appointment with someone, is it in your agenda? Ideally, you entered it in your agenda when you made the appointment, and you entered any task or activity you committed to in your To-Do list.

Patrick had committed to rekindle his marriage. He adds a task to organize an interesting date with his wife and blocks off Saturday evening. He's also committed to taking over grocery shopping and laundry; he adds these tasks to his To-Do list. Eventually this will become a routine that is recurrent on his agenda.

IMPROVE YOUR TIME ESTIMATIONS

As mentioned earlier, Creative Geniuses struggle to estimate how long it takes to accomplish a task. When estimating the duration of a task you've never done before, use this rule of thumb: triple your first guess.

Once you've practiced a task enough so that your time estimates are more accurate, you can use that figure instead, but only for that task. Always leave yourself a time buffer when planning time for a task. It's best to under-promise and over-deliver. Write the estimated time required to do the task in your To-Do List beside the task.

Note the deadlines for any task and consider them in your planning. Sonia knows that one of the two proposals must be in the client's hands by Wednesday so she writes this deadline in her To-Do List and treats this task first.

With a filtered and clarified To-Do List, you can now continue your quest to master self-management by setting up your agenda.

MANAGE YOUR AGENDA

A To-Do list is worthless until you commit your tasks to your agenda. That's the only way you complete them. To book tasks in your agenda, follow these steps:

1. Consider your energy levels – John blocks off mornings in his agenda to avoid being scheduled by colleagues for meetings during his peak time. He'll later fill the blocks with task that optimize his mornings.

2. Commit to routine self-care – Committed to exercising in the morning, Patrick sets 10 pm as his bedtime so he can get the seven hours of sleep he requires to optimize his concentration. He also adds a routine for arriving home that includes changing out of work clothes, replenishing his gym bag and depositing his things (keys, bus pass, wallet and agenda) in a caddy on his dresser. Until this routine is well established, he sets a daily reminder in his agenda that will ring an alarm on his PDA around the time he usually arrives home. However, once his system has become a habit, he is able to forgo the alarms, as he executes his system automatically. Sonia schedules every Friday morning for planning.

3. Honor previous commitments – Sonia scans her agenda to ensure

she's met all of her commitments from the previous week. She notices two tasks she had scheduled but didn't complete. She adds them to her To-Do List.

4. Maximize your strengths and interests – Review your strengths and interests and consider adding activities during the week that will further develop something from that list. Sonia has always imagined herself addressing crowds of people. This is one of the motivations behind her dream of being a role model for young women entrepreneurs everywhere. To pursue this interest, she decides to find and contact a Toastmaster's group that meets at a convenient time and place.

5. Schedule tasks from your filtered To-Do list – Go through your To-Do list and commit each activity to your agenda, taking care to consider the task characteristics and energy levels to maximize your efficiency and effectiveness.

6. Once you've scheduled a task in your agenda, if you are able to book sufficient time to complete the task, cross it off your To-Do list. If a task is so long (and you're sure it's a task and not a project!) that you can't schedule it all at once, leave the task on your To Do List, but subtract the time from the task to reduce the time remaining to schedule in your agenda.

John worries that scheduling his To-Do list into his agenda will box him in, but despite his misgivings, and with encouragement, he decides to try it.

I encourage you to be patient. I know this may be difficult, but you won't need to wait long to see results. In fact, rather than patience, I ask that you have faith. It's a case of "Try it, you'll like it." Each step will help you on your quest for sustainable self-management. On faith, John completes all the steps in the planning process. He soon finds he makes better use of his peak times and realizes that scheduling tasks according to his energy patterns allows him to shave hours off the time required to complete each task, and makes it so much more enjoyable to do because he isn't fighting his brain. Taking advantage of his energy patterns is a critical step in his self-management.

He is also better able to honor his commitments with his colleagues; he feels more in control instead of less in control.

Finally, to truly master self-control, you must act as your own agent, directing your career (and your life) toward projects and activities that allow you to use your best assets and that you are passionate about. The best results are that you have more time and energy to invest in developing your strengths and interests.

TO TRULY MASTER SELF-CONTROL, YOU MUST ACT AS YOUR OWN AGENT, DIRECTING YOUR CAREER (AND YOUR LIFE) TOWARD PROJECTS AND ACTIVITIES THAT ALLOW YOU TO USE YOUR BEST ASSETS AND THAT YOU ARE PASSIONATE ABOUT.

As you take charge, you'll advance in your career or business, improve your relationships with friends and family and manage the many things that sustain you with ease. You'll be healthier, have clarity and feel in control, plus you'll feel more self-confident, credible and able to make more (considered) choices because you're justifiably confident in your abilities.

Taking charge will feel uncomfortable at times (if it doesn't, you're not stretching and will never achieve your full potential.) You'll be tempted to return to your old ways, but before you do that, consider the people you love and who love you. Will you let them down? Even more importantly, will you let yourself down? Resistance is a normal part of every worthwhile endeavor. We'll discuss ways to overcome your resistance in the next two chapters.

When you're tempted to revert to your old ways or worse, to

give up, consider going back to your dream and finding an activity that will allow you to relive the passion that started you on this path. What is the really important, compelling reason you want to do this?

You're reading this book because you want to change your life. You can't keep doing the same thing but expect different results. You are a Creative Genius. I believe you can lead a fulfilling and happy life by developing your strengths, creating systems to overcome your weaknesses and tapping into the innate abilities of your passionate mind.

CONCLUSION

When you plan for success, you're much more likely to achieve it. Starting from a "big picture" view of your life, then setting goals and identifying projects, routines and systems that will take you there are only the first steps. Taking charge of your To-Dos and your projects, and using your agenda to schedule your commitments to others, but more importantly to yourself, allow you to put your plan in motion and reach your goals.

TO LEAD A FULFILLING AND HAPPY LIFE, DEVELOP YOUR STRENGTHS, CREATE SYSTEMS TO OVERCOME YOUR WEAKNESSES AND TAP INTO THE INNATE ABILITIES OF YOUR PASSIONATE MIND.

In the next section we'll discuss ways to overcome resistance and procrastination and to get others on board, ready and willing to help you.

|||||||||||||||||||||||||
KEY POINTS

✦ You need quarterly and annual planning sessions to

- Take stock of your achievements and lessons learned
- Celebrate
- Prepare for the coming year

✦ On a monthly basis

- Review projects
- Adjust your course

✦ On a weekly basis

- Review and manage project tasks
- Update your To-Do list with the next steps in projects
- Review and update your Not-To-Do
- Filter your To-Do list
- Schedule tasks in your agenda

✦ Manage your agenda

- Consider your energy levels when scheduling tasks
- Commit to routine self-care in your agenda up front
- Decide on a routine time for planning
- Honor previous but incomplete commitments
- Maximize the use of your strengths and interests
- Filter your To-Do list
- Schedule tasks in your agenda

If you feel you'd like to get into action right now to build your dream, visit Master Self-Control at **www.TimetobeCreative. com.**

For additional information and support, visit Coach Linda Walker at **www.CoachLindaWalker.com.**

PART FIVE. TAKE CHARGE – CONCLUSION

The last two chapters allowed you to create the tools you'll use in your "You" management system and to see the types of planning practices that play to your Creative Genius brain and allows you to put into action what you need to do to achieve your goals and honor your vision.

If you feel you're ready to learn how to plan your time and your life more effectively, visit Master Self-Control at www.TimetobeCreative.com.

For additional information and support, visit Coach Linda Walker at www.CoachLindaWalker.com.

PART SIX
PAVE THE WAY FOR CHANGE

CHAPTER 20
Conquer Procrastination Now

CHAPTER 21
Get Everyone on board

PART SIX. PAVE THE WAY FOR CHANGE— INTRODUCTION

A word of caution; changing your patterns and routines requires work. You resist change; we all do, and we often do it in the form of procrastination. In Chapter 20, we'll help you plow through your resistance and conquer procrastination. Everyone resists change, but because you're doing it for a good reason, and you know the change will make your life better, you'll do whatever it takes. However, when your changes affect other people, they'll resist the changes even more than you! You can avoid many problems by explaining the changes you'll be making before you make them, and especially by taking time to share why you're making these changes.

We'll discuss the steps to ensure the buy-in and support of those around you in Chapter 21.

CHAPTER TWENTY

||||||||||||||||||||||||||||||||||||||

CONQUER PROCRASTINATION NOW

Most people procrastinate. They occasionally put off things until later, tomorrow, next week or never. That's normal; we're not talking about that type of procrastination. Your procrastination has gotten you into trouble repeatedly. Your procrastination has put you in embarrassing situations, has cost you financially and has even cost you in your relationships. And you can be sure it will continue to do so until you learn to overcome it.

Procrastination is one of the worst self-management obstacles because it compounds every other productivity and time management challenge resulting in inconsistent performance, tardiness, missed deadlines and dishonored commitments.

PROCRASTINATION IS ONE OF THE WORST SELF-MANAGEMENT OBSTACLES BECAUSE IT COMPOUNDS EVERY OTHER PRODUCTIVITY AND TIME MANAGEMENT CHALLENGE.

To truly conquer procrastination, we must go beyond mere tricks and dig out the root of the problem. Like weeds, getting at the roots is the only way you can finally erase procrastination from your life.

TO TRULY CONQUER PROCRASTINATION, WE MUST GO BEYOND
MERE TRICKS AND DIG OUT THE ROOT OF THE PROBLEM.

In this chapter, we'll identify the various sources of procrastination and discuss solutions that get right to the root of the problem. We'll delve into the procrastination issues Patrick, John and
Sonia face, as they're sure to be similar to your own. We'll define
what they are procrastinating, identify what it is about these activities that has them procrastinating, to get to the source of the
problem and then we'll resolve the issue by attacking the problem
at its source.

BENEFITS OF PROCRASTINATION

Why do you keep procrastinating? Despite the cost, the payoff
for procrastinating is very attractive. Ignoring long-term consequences, procrastination frees you from doing something you'd
rather not do and allows you to do something else, something
more interesting or fun, instead. Even better, the payoff is instan-
taneous. You reap the "rewards" of procrastinating immediately,
whereas assuming your responsibilities and honoring your commitments pays off in the comparably distant future.

TRADITIONAL STRATEGIES CAN'T WORK FOR
CREATIVE GENIUSES

People who rarely procrastinate typically dismiss it as a seri-
ous problem and tell sufferers to follow *Nike*'s advice. However,
"just do it," is not very helpful advice for chronic procrastinators.
When this approach doesn't work, people usually turn to one of
three popular strategies to "cure" their procrastination:

+ Do the most important task first. People who are motivated by importance will respond to this approach, building momentum to carry through and complete not only the important task, but also the less vital tasks that follow it. However, as a Creative Genius, importance doesn't activate your brain, interest does.

✦ Do the hardest task first. People who procrastinate because they lack energy can accomplish more by doing the hardest tasks while they are fresh and tackle progressively easier tasks as their energy diminishes. As a Creative Genius, your energy levels fluctuate dramatically, making such a linear approach ineffective.

✦ Whatever the task, do it now. People capable of transitioning easily between activities can deal with small distractions and return to what they were doing. This frees their mind from worry about the many "emergencies" that come up every day. As a Creative Genius, one of your "superpowers" is that you are able to achieve such an intense level of clarity and focus people refer to it as "hyper-focus." However, that means you lose more productive time to distraction-caused transitions than any other single factor.

Each of these approaches fails to address key characteristics of the way your brain works.

CONQUER PROCRASTINATION STEP BY STEP

Can you conquer procrastination? Yes. But the strategy you choose must match the true source of the procrastination for each activity you procrastinate. You must:

1. Identify and define what you are procrastinating
2. Identify the root cause of the procrastination
3. Attack the source of the procrastination

DEFINE WHAT YOU ARE PROCRASTINATING

Most people would say "duh! That's not difficult – I already know what I can't get done." However, most activities you engage in are a series of tasks; and while the whole activity may be halted, it is usually one specific task you are procrastinating.

To define what you are procrastinating, you'll have to dig deeper:

1. Break up the activity into tasks;
2. Consider how you feel about each task; and
3. Consider how you feel about the results

BREAK UP THE ACTIVITIES INTO TASKS

One of my clients was procrastinating writing an essay. We broke up the process of writing an essay and found that while she had no problems deciding what to write about or researching the topic (actually, she loved research), the task that stopped her in her tracks was organizing her thoughts.

Sonia puts off writing her proposals. She breaks the process into tasks. Among the steps defining the end project is her favorite. As a visionary thinker, visualizing the end results is one of Sonia's strengths. She doesn't mind describing each step of the project once she's defined her vision or researching and pricing the cost of supplies and rental of equipment; many of these require her to meet or speak to others, which she loves to do. Other steps include estimating the cost of labor required, writing and formatting the document, then delivering it to the client.

HOW DO YOU FEEL ABOUT EACH TASK?

When you choose to do something because it is fun, you look forward to doing it or if you greatly anticipate the results, your tendency to procrastinate will diminish. It will be more present if it is something you hate to do or you are "forced" to do.

When you contemplate the task, are you thinking about how

good it will be to get it over with, or is your focus on how painful it will be to do the task? Thinking about the pain rather than the reward increases your chances of procrastinating. If thoughts of the reward are not sufficient to distract you from the pain, some "dream building" can help you focus on the goal rather than the obstacles.

In writing proposals, Sonia hates estimating how much labor will be required, writing all the legal parts and formatting the proposal. She is not a detail-oriented person (most Creative Geniuses are not), but is still a bit of a perfectionist.

Creative Geniuses are interest-based performers. Your brain doesn't energize when tackling boring tasks. Imagine your brain is the motor in your car; as much as you might want your car to move, if the motor isn't running, you're not going anywhere. This is one time when being a Creative Genius doesn't help.

Even if you really, really, want to do something, when you find the task boring, you struggle because your brain doesn't ignite. Task importance is irrelevant in igniting your brain, as is the importance of the person requesting that you do the task. Yes, you recognize importance and you're more than willing to complete important tasks. But if the task is boring, you struggle. You need your brain to be awake to get anything done.

HOW DO YOU FEEL ABOUT THE RESULTS?

If you don't want the results, you may be putting off the activity to avoid them rather than because of the task. Patrick's household responsibilities are minimal. He is responsible for getting the car repaired, repairing things around the house, and calling contractors as needed.

He is far from handy but he feels that as "man of the house," he has to be in charge of renovations and repairs. Sometimes, you do things because someone else decides you should. Other times, you choose to do things because "that's what's expected."

Patrick could only focus on the chaos and disarray that ensued whenever he thinks of renovating. He leaves projects half done because he hits a problem he doesn't know how to solve. The messes that lay in the wake of his numerous unfinished projects create a lot of anxiety for him and his wife; he can't relax.

Sonia procrastinates her proposals. She's frustrated because she knows that the more proposals she completes, the more will be accepted to ultimately increase her revenues. So it is clear that the results are not part of the problem.

IDENTIFY THE ROOT CAUSE OF THE PROCRASTINATION

In completing step 1, that is, defining specifically what task or tasks of your activity you are procrastinating, you may have already defined the problem and found a solution. We'll delve into the most common sources of procrastination and provide solutions that hit at the heart of each one.

CONQUERING YOUR LACK OF INTEREST

Patrick's original coaching objective is to "be normal." He wants to pull his weight at home and get his work done efficiently and effectively. We work on developing his dream of becoming an artist to help motivate him, but some issues are more urgent.

He resolves many of his work issues through better self-management. Using his self-management system, taking advantage of his energy patterns, using routines and systems and using his strengths whenever possible made him far more effective at work. However, his home life is still challenging. Patrick puts off his chores, or forgets them completely. His wife is discouraged and tired of filling both adult pairs of shoes in the family.

She is flabbergasted at the latest incident catastrophe. She had asked him to call their mechanic to get a noise in the car checked a few months earlier. He'd seemed sincere when he said he'd do it, but now, three months later, she is at the garage checking on the noise that has only gotten worse, just to discover Patrick has never gotten the problem checked. It will now cost $1200 to fix. The mechanic tells her that if they'd come when the problem first started it would have cost no more than $300. She tells Patrick she feels she can't count on him for any help because he never follows through and she has lost any trust in him. The truth stings.

When we break up the project of getting the car fixed into tasks, I ask how he feels about each task required to accomplish this work, he says he has never been interested in sports, cars, power tools or home renovations. Furthermore, he isn't comfortable talking to people on the phone or face-to-face; he especially hates conversations around these topics.

Lack of interest is one of the most common reasons people procrastinate. Sonia, our entrepreneur, struggles to prepare her invoices because she finds most of the tasks boring. While the result might be enticing, the actual activity bores her to tears.

John also struggles with boredom. Some reports he has to produce at work bore him. He waits until the last minute to complete them, using his adrenaline to help him focus. It's not that he doesn't try to complete the task before the deadline. He enters it in his agenda ahead of time but when he tries to follow his plan, he finds himself easily distracted by his thoughts.

SOLUTIONS TO PROCRASTINATION DUE TO LACK OF INTEREST

You have several options for conquering procrastination when caused by lack of interest. You can barter it, delegate it, drop it or delay it. You can also use momentum. For Patrick we decide to use the first two of these solutions.

BARTERING

Before our next session, Patrick agrees to ask his wife which chores she finds particularly difficult. Together, they will select a few chores he can take over for her. She explains that grocery shopping is physically draining for her. He asks her to take over any communication with other parties, such as the plumber or the mechanic. In exchange, he will be in charge of grocery shopping. They also determine he will share in the laundry and cleaning. His wife enjoys talking to people and he doesn't mind lugging groceries around.

DELEGATING

When I discuss delegating tasks my clients find boring, most feel they can't because they're at the bottom of the totem pole or because they don't have enough money to pay someone to do those things. However, you can delegate to systems as well.

DELEGATING TO SYSTEMS

To plan how he will do the groceries, Patrick uses his strengths. He is particularly adept at creating systems, so he uses this skill to create a menu, make a list and systematically go through the grocery store, aisle by aisle, to pick up the items on his list. His wife, who is sure the family will starve to death waiting for Patrick to get around to doing the groceries, is pleasantly surprised when he schedules it in his agenda and actually completes it consistently every week. In effect, Patrick delegates the grocery shopping to a system. In only a few weeks, he streamlines the process so much that within 60 minutes, he is home again with a week's worth of groceries.

Sonia also delegates to a system. Even better, she even delegated creating the system to someone! She hired a person to develop a template she could use to streamline her invoicing process. Now, once she enters the name, address and costing in the original proposal, that same information automatically carries over to her contracts, her invoicing and even her Change Request forms. Automation is one the least expensive and best ways of delegating to system.

DELEGATING TO SOMEONE ELSE

Sonia quickly realizes that her strengths are her visionary thinking and communication skills. Once she has her invoicing system complete, she is ready to grow her business even bigger, so she delegates it to a virtual assistant.

INJECT INTEREST, NOVELTY, COMPETITION, INTRIGUE AND SOMETIMES URGENCY,

Sometimes, even when you manage to barter or delegate the tasks that create problems, there will be activities you just can't delegate or drop. In these cases, the ideal solution is to inject interest into the task. You do that by finding a different way of doing the task that's more interesting.

INJECT INTEREST INTO THE TASK BY FINDING A DIFFERENT WAY OF DOING THE TASK THAT'S MORE INTERESTING.

Patrick and his wife clarify their respective responsibilities for cleaning the house. Patrick vacuums and washes the floors after his wife dusts and cleans the kitchen and bathroom. Unfortunately, there is always something else more interesting than vacuuming or washing the floors.

Patrick loves music so he injects interest by playing loud music as he vacuums. Using novelty to generate interest is also a powerful way to overcome procrastination. You can inject novelty by changing the order in which you do things, by doing it somewhere else or at a different period in the day.

USING NOVELTY TO GENERATE INTEREST IS ALSO A POWERFUL WAY TO OVERCOME PROCRASTINATION.

Add competition using a timer; try to beat your best time or compete with someone else who is doing the same thing. The possibility of a prize in the end can also add interest.

You can add interest if you inject intrigue, particularly around report writing or information gathering by asking questions and investigating. One client writing an essay noted questions she might have regarding the subject she was writing about and then she treated it as an investigation and she reported on her findings.

Urgency tends to be the standard strategy for most Creative Geniuses. You wait until the last minute to tap into the adrenaline rising from the fear of not finishing on time. It's tempting because it's very effective but in the long term, this can annoy people counting on you and can even cause health issues.

Patrick opts for a combination of these solutions. First, he uses competition to see how quickly he can vacuum, trying to beat his time each week. In addition, he plays music and sings at the top of his lungs as he washes the floors. These strategies work well for Patrick and he is able to meet his responsibilities.

Creative Geniuses really struggle to activate their brain around tasks they find boring, and when they can't activate their brains, they are easily distracted by their own thoughts or by things that happen around them.

USE MOMENTUM

When you're not interested, your brain doesn't engage, making any activity that requires focus, concentration and use of your executive functions daunting. Is it any wonder you put those activities off as long as possible? Each time you attempt a boring task you're easily distracted. Often, the only way to accomplish a task is to wait until the last minute, substituting a feeling of urgency (which can temporarily activate your brain) for interest. Whenever possible, avoid tasks or activities you don't find interesting.

Momentum can also help you do a boring task that's necessary and that you can't delegate. Use momentum to ignite your brain so that you can focus. Start with a relatively short task that gives you energy; once your brain ignites, move on to the boring task. When your energy wanes, switch back to an interesting task, gain momentum and switch back.

This is what John does to get his reports started. He goes for a walk in the office; the exercise helps wake up his brain. He gets to his cubicle and starts working on the report. As soon as he feels the momentum dropping, he sets a timer for 15 minutes and chats with someone, something he enjoys doing. He then returns to work, usually sustaining his focus longer each time. Often after two or three interludes, he's managed to get his report done.

USE A BODY DOUBLE

A body double is someone who is present, though not engaged with you, while you work. This person could be doing something different from what you're doing, and they should not disturb you. The body double technique helps many of my clients, particularly those with ADHD. It's not clear why it works so well, but it has proven very effective.

John uses a body double, working with a colleague who, like him, also struggles with his expense reports. They'd get together in a meeting room and work away. They don't talk to each other or interact. They both usually stay on task until their reports are complete.

CONQUERING YOUR DECISION-MAKING PROBLEMS

Decision-making requires that you clarify the problem, prioritize a list of criteria for your decision and assign a weight to each criterion, list possible solutions and select the right one. It's a long process with many potential pitfalls.

Struggling to make decisions can be a daily issue for many Creative Geniuses. The feelings of overwhelm and frustration you feel working through the decision-making process leads you to make impulsive decisions or to avoid them altogether.

Common complaints of clients with decision-making problems include not knowing where to start, lacking sufficient information to make the "right" (read a "perfect") decision and having too many options to choose from.

YOU DON'T KNOW WHERE TO START

Creative Geniuses often procrastinate when they feel overwhelmed. This indicates a problem with prioritizing or sequencing tasks or projects. You have great ideas and you easily become excited about all of them. Deciding which to tackle first can paralyze you.

CREATIVE GENIUSES OFTEN PROCRASTINATE WHEN THEY FEEL OVERWHELMED. THIS INDICATES A PROBLEM WITH PRIORITIZING OR SEQUENCING TASKS OR PROJECTS.

John struggles with an issue common for adults with ADHD: he struggles to organize, plan and prioritize. Without knowing what is more important, he can't decide what to start first. To make matters worse, his colleagues constantly dump "urgent" tasks on him.

Many Creative Geniuses, anticipating interruptions, simply don't start any task requiring concentrated effort but wait for interruptions to give them something to do. An attractive trap, it frequently affects entrepreneurs; you feel productive and people appreciate you when you solve their problems. Soon, however, you're not reaching your own objectives because you never get any of your own work done. In fact, you've handed control of your schedule to anyone who walks in your office or calls you.

YOU LACK INFORMATION OR KNOWLEDGE

Often procrastination results from trying to make the perfect decision. Moving forward is impossible until you decide, and your perfectionism keeps you from doing just that. Unable to decide that your work is good enough or that you're finished it, keeps you in perpetual 'fine-tuning' mode.

TOO MANY OPTIONS AVAILABLE

Creative Geniuses are often excited by their ideas and the numerous opportunities they spot. Sonia also struggles with procrastination because she has too many ideas, especially for marketing her business. Every day reveals yet another exciting possibility. She is soon overwhelmed and unable to decide which of her brilliant ideas to implement.

At times, you procrastinate because you can't decide if or when you want to do something. John often toys with whether to work out or not. When he decides to do it, he then struggles to decide when he should do it. Sonia goes through the same dilemma every week, deciding whether or not to attend a networking session.

Making a decision is a complex process, but it doesn't need to be an obstacle to your success.

SOLUTIONS TO DECISION-MAKING PROBLEMS
PRIORITIZE BASED ON THE SITUATION

Prioritizing is essential for decision-making. However, it can be difficult to identify the right criteria to use to prioritize, so selecting ways to prioritize based on the situation can help resolve the problem.

For example, John can use the deadline for each task in his endless To-Do List and prioritize them according to urgency. In the long run this is not the best way to prioritize since this fails to take into account how long each task takes and the best time to do it.

Using Urgency to make decisions about what to do next keeps you in "Firefighter mode." While the adrenaline your body generates in this mode may help you concentrate, it damages your health over time, not to mention its impact on your family and social life as you work late to complete last-minute tasks.

John confides that he often works through the night, once even working 36 hours straight without sleep, food, or going home in order to finish an important task he'd procrastinated for months.

Importance makes a better criterion for your decision. Importance is the impact a task has on you and others around you. Consider the following:

+ How critical is the project or task to reaching personal or organizational goals?
+ What's the impact of procrastinating? Who will be affected, and how?

While making decisions based on urgency or importance can provide some guidance, many Creative Geniuses still struggle to start even an important task if it is not interesting. Earlier in this chapter, we discussed how to counter this using momentum to activate your brain when working on an important but uninteresting task.

WHILE MAKING DECISIONS BASED ON URGENCY OR
IMPORTANCE CAN PROVIDE SOME GUIDANCE, MANY
CREATIVE GENIUSES STILL STRUGGLE TO START EVEN AN
IMPORTANT TASK IF IT IS NOT INTERESTING.

PRE-PROGRAM YOUR DECISIONS

Of all the solutions to decision-making problems, the one I advocate most is limiting unnecessary decisions. Many people remake a decision numerous times. For example, John decides each day whether to go to the gym or not, and then he decides when to go. Sonia revisits her decision whether or not to attend a networking event. Each time, they face the same struggle with the decision-making process. This robs you of time and energy, which you can avoid by limiting the number of decisions you need to make. Simply reuse good decisions many times.

Preprogrammed decisions such as routines, patterns, systems and habits are powerful tools that allow Creative Geniuses to improve their productivity by simplifying or eliminating many of the decisions each of us must make daily.

Using preprogrammed templates and delegating to systems and routines will also alleviate your decision-making headaches.

PREPROGRAMMED DECISIONS SUCH AS ROUTINES, PATTERNS,
SYSTEMS AND HABITS ARE POWERFUL TOOLS THAT ALLOW
CREATIVE GENIUSES TO IMPROVE THEIR PRODUCTIVITY.

CREATE ROUTINES

You can reduce the number and frequency of decisions you make every day by creating routines to support the decisions you've already made. John does exactly that. Once he decides he wants and needs to go to the gym every day, he decides when he plans to go each day. With practice, it becomes automatic for him to go to the gym at the right time. Sonia decides which networking groups yield the best results, finalizes a list of networking events she will attend and sticks to it.

Routines are a great way to reduce decision-making. When you create routines, you make a decision once and implement it numerous times. Take the time to make a good decision, weighing the pros and cons, and then, once you've made your best decision, reuse that decision many times.

USING A DECISION TEMPLATE

It's impossible to make the perfect decision. There is an endless amount of information available, you have perceptual biases, which distort the problem and solutions and you face time and money constraints.

IT'S IMPOSSIBLE TO MAKE THE PERFECT DECISION.

It is beyond the capacity of one person to assimilate the ever-burgeoning amount of information available, let alone to organize, prioritize and evaluate that information. Furthermore, new information becomes available constantly, making it impossible to assess all the information you need to make a perfect decision.

Instead, construct a simplified model that incorporates only the essential features of the problem. Define the problem by its most obvious parameters, identify a limited set of factors and consider a limited number of alternatives. It's usually best to consider only the factors you can influence. You can also limit the alternative solutions you consider and limit the information you collect. Finally, set a time limit for making your decision and budget for the cost of the solution. A satisfactory decision will result and though it is not a perfect decision, it is preferable to eternal procrastination.

Many Creative Geniuses refer to this as "going with your gut," though they are really using their knowledge and experience to construct the necessary models subconsciously.

When choosing between several ways to market her business, Sonia uses a decision template. She identifies and weighs different criteria, lists the possible options, scores each possible solution according to each criterion, multiplies each score by the weight of the criterion and then adds all the weighted scores so she is able to identify her top three options. It sounds complicated but it isn't. You can use this model Decision Matrix by accessing the members' only area at www.coachlindawalker.com/WithTimeToSpare. By using a decision template, she limits her choices and the criteria she most consider when making the decisions.

Decision templates can help overcome your decision-making perfectionism; however, there are times when perfectionism stems from a limiting belief and requires a deeper intervention. We'll address this later in this chapter.

DELEGATING TO SYSTEMS

Even without a computer, you can program decisions. Creating rules and policies are all ways of programming decisions. You limit the number of necessary decisions by creating systems or workflows that incorporate decisions you've made in the past. You can even delegate some types of decision-making to a system by creating a clear, pre-defined decision-making process.

CREATE A CLEAR PROCESS

Patrick's company is involved in thousands of project each year. Fewer than 100 of these projects need to be fully investigated, but which ones? The process for choosing which projects need the full treatment must be focused and precise to ensure all qualified projects are identified. He creates a quick and effective process for qualifying projects for intervention by interviewing project managers ahead of time.

He develops a set of questions designed to test the criteria required for his department to get involved. This reduces the time his department devotes to unqualified projects while ensuring no qualifying projects are missed.

CONQUER PROCRASTINATION DUE TO PLANNING PROBLEMS

Many Creative Geniuses struggle to plan. Planning is a complex process requiring that you identify steps in a project and then sequence and prioritize them. Visionary Creative Geniuses often visualize projects as a finished "product," so identifying all these steps can be daunting.

Planning problems often occur when you

+ Have difficulty organizing your thoughts or knowing where to start
+ Need to shift your focus from "big picture" to details frequently
+ Find the project too complicated with too many "moving parts."
+ First, we'll consider each of these planning problems separately and then we'll look at solutions for resolving them.

DIFFICULTY ORGANIZING YOUR THOUGHTS

When Sonia knows she has a proposal to write, she cringes. She knows it means hours of work and worse, hours of trying to figure out where to start. She is unable to organize her thoughts. As a result, she tends to wait until the last minute or not complete them at all.

The large number of tasks he juggles on his To-Do list also often overwhelms John. He creates a list but never accomplishes anything on it. Not knowing where to start, he allows urgent tasks to distract him in order to avoid planning his day.

LACK OF CLARITY

Lack of skills, knowledge or the resources required for the task, or your perception that you lack them often leads to procrastination. You may feel you need to know everything there is about a task before you attempt it. Most people forget that we learn by making mistakes. You learned to walk, to talk, to read and to write by trying, making mistakes and improving a little at a time.

You may also lack the information you need because you fail to clarify the expected result. This often happens because of your eagerness to please or of your excitement about a project.

Patrick's issue is not clarifying the criteria for success. In one example, he must create a couple of PowerPoint slides to illustrate a set of data. He cannot decide what format to use. He realizes he didn't have all the information he needed to complete the assignment, so he stares at his computer for hours, trying to figure out what to do next. The lack of clarity makes it difficult for him to decide how to present the data (In a table? A bar graph? A pie chart?) or what data to present (All data together? Or separate sets?). In his haste to accept the project, he'd forgotten to ask for sufficient details and now, days into the project, he is embarrassed to ask for the information he should have had before he began.

SHIFTING YOUR FOCUS

Entrepreneurs, authors, adults with ADHD and other Creative Geniuses facing very large projects often describe their procrastination as originating from a feeling of overwhelm. However, there are times when overwhelm can indicate a different cause of procrastination. Sonia sets the vision for her company, but as the only administrative staff in her organization, she also must to deal with executing details such as invoicing, filing tax reports and tracking the minutia of her project plans.

She finds shifting her focus from "Big Picture" to the details of everyday activities to be very difficult. Even in her marketing efforts, she sets the strategy but she also needs to execute her plan. This constant movement from Big Picture (or visionary) thinking to detail-oriented thinking makes planning difficult because each shift requires a difficult transition; sometimes she'll be thinking tactics when she needs a vision and vice versa.

IT'S TOO COMPLICATED

Lengthy or complex tasks are potential sources of procrastination. When a task is complicated, even if you know how to deal with it, you hate the aggravation it will cause. Finding several consecutive hours in a day to complete a lengthy or complex task can also prove difficult.

Creative Geniuses often find themselves with a To-Do List that mixes (and confuses) projects and tasks. If you can break an item on your To-Do List into multiple steps, it is not a task but a project and it doesn't belong on your To-Do list. Attempting to complete a project without breaking it into steps is like trying to eat a whole pie in one gulp… it can't be done. Where do you start? It's only after you've broken the project (or cut the pie) into smaller pieces that it becomes manageable.

IF YOU CAN BREAK AN ITEM ON YOUR TO-DO LIST INTO MULTIPLE STEPS, IT IS NOT A TASK BUT A PROJECT, AND IT DOESN'T BELONG ON YOUR TO-DO LIST.

YOU HAVE A PLANNING PROBLEM

Creative Geniuses are their own biggest planning problem, as they often prefer "doing" to "thinking." They may not plan at all, as is the case with John and his endless To-Do list.

If you mistake projects for tasks and find you can't organize your thoughts, or constantly shifting from strategy to tactics leaves you with no coherent plan, you have a planning problem. Luckily, the solutions tend to be easy to understand and easy to implement.

SOLUTIONS TO PLANNING PROBLEMS
CLARIFY THE RESPONSIBILITIES

Patrick's success with grocery shopping does not spill over into his other responsibilities: sharing the laundry and cleaning the house with his wife. He mentions a fight he'd had with his wife one morning because he had no clean underwear. Livid, his wife asked him why he did not put a load of laundry through when he'd pulled out his last pair of underwear the morning before. He had to admit, she was right.

I challenge him to take the laundry over completely, explaining that the problem seems to be a lack of clarity over expectations. As long as he shares the laundry with his wife, he never knows where her responsibility ends and his begins. Once he takes over the full responsibility for this task, he makes it a recurrent task in his agenda and completes it as scheduled.

PRACTICE GOOD SELF-MANAGEMENT

One solution to the never-ending To-Do list is to use Project Task Lists. If you recall in Chapter 19 we suggest you only list in your To-Do list those To-Dos you must complete in the next week; tasks for future weeks or months stay on their respective Project Task Lists until you are ready to work on them. In addition, when you move tasks off your To-Do list to book them in your agenda, scheduling each task in your agenda based on your energy patterns will make a huge improvement in your productivity. Choosing the right time to complete tasks makes the work easier.

John has been preparing his To-Do list but he resists scheduling tasks in his agenda because he feels it will stifle his creativity. Since his agenda is free, he finds himself available to help others put out fires but he never gets to his tasks until the last minute.

Realizing that not planning his time allows anyone to interrupt and pull him away from what he needs to do, and that working late or in last-minute rushes does more to stifle his creativity than imposing some structure to his time, he commits to planning his tasks in his agenda and following his plan. He soon finds his full agenda acts as armor plating, protecting him from interruptions and additional assignments. He doesn't feel guilty saying no when he can point to his packed agenda as his reason for refusing.

CLARIFY THE PROBLEM OR THE INTENDED RESULTS

When accepting a new assignment, be clear on what people expect you to accomplish. Prepare your list of questions before you discuss the project. Since these are often the same questions, create a template. The list of questions below will help you avoid being caught in a project where you're not exactly sure what you're trying to accomplish.

WHEN ACCEPTING A NEW ASSIGNMENT, BE CLEAR ON WHAT PEOPLE EXPECT YOU TO ACCOMPLISH.

You need to know:
+ What exactly are the expected results?
+ What is the format they want the results presented in? (a chart, a table, etc.)

+ How specific or accurate does it need to be?
+ When is the deadline? Why choose this deadline?
+ What is the purpose of the project?
+ Who are the stakeholders (the people counting on the results)?
+ How do these results fit within the overall project?

Faced with preparing a status report for his boss, Patrick sets his pride aside and meets with his boss to clarify the intended results for his PowerPoint presentation. He learns what results to incorporate into his report and how the results need to be presented. After fretting for days about this assignment, once he knows the specifics, it takes less than two hours to complete.

PROJECTS VS. TASKS

As you may have realized, Sonia's proposals are not tasks but projects. To complete one proposal, she must determine the intended results, identify the milestones, then the tasks, determine the number of hours and required resources and calculate the cost of resources, supplies and equipment usage and rental. Finally, she must format it, print it and deliver it to the client.

As soon as Sonia realizes this, she is able to create a proposal template that includes each of these steps. By breaking it down, it becomes obvious where she needs to start. As an added benefit, she is able to delegate part of the process, the formatting, to a virtual assistant.

Once you realize that a given To-Do is not a To-Do (or task) but multiple tasks or a project, the next step is to break it into steps or into sub-projects (for big projects). Milestones mark the end of mini- or sub-projects within a big project. For example, renovating a bathroom would include sub-projects such as gutting the bathroom, modifying the rough plumbing, tiling and installing bathroom "appliances." Each of these is a project consisting of multiple tasks that, combined, make up a larger project.

EXTERNALIZE YOUR THOUGHTS

Externalizing your thoughts means getting them out of your head where they tend to bounce around like pin balls and onto some external place. Several strategies can help organize your thoughts about a large project with many potential approaches. These include:

Mind mapping (see Tony Buzan's book, How to Mind Map) to create an outline or a list of milestones and steps,

✦ Talking it over with someone you trust and asking them to help you identify the main parts of what you are trying to accomplish.
✦ Asking a friend to interview you about the project and record the conversation. Have the recording transcribed or listen to it as you write, and break the project into phases.
✦ Writing a description of the steps you would take.

Each of these strategies helps to externalize the organization process. They permit you to step "out of your head" so you can examine your thoughts objectively.

Sonia finds that mind mapping is an excellent tool for her marketing development. It helps her see the big picture. She is better able to identify what strategies, plans and tactics are required to support her big picture.

ASK FOR HELP

Often, other people determine your priorities. Your boss, your spouse, your clients and your co-workers all have an opinion as to which of your many tasks or projects are high priority. When you're uncertain about which task or project you should do first, ask.

At work, it is a good idea to confirm your priorities frequently. Your boss will want you to do tasks in order of importance, and in many companies, the relative importance of tasks changes frequently in response to market fluctuations, client requests and even office politics.

When John's boss asks him to produce a report on short notice, he realizes it risks delaying a deliverable he must complete by the end of the day. He asks his boss to confirm the priority and delivery date of the report. He soon discovers his boss does not really need the report as quickly as he'd made it seem.

COMPARTMENTALIZE

Like many Creative Geniuses, Sonia struggles with shifting focus. We devise a new strategy of compartmentalizing her different roles and using Time Boxing to delineate when she will tackle Big Picture thinking and days when she'll deal with details and execution. Time Boxing is a high-level view of planning that predetermines and limits the time you will spend dealing with each area of your life. Sonia uses Monday morning as Big Picture Thinking time; Monday afternoon is for connecting with clients and prospects, Monday evening she takes an art class, Tuesday morning is Proposal Writing time and so on.

When Sonia does her planning in her agenda, she divides the Big Picture activities from the Detail activities and allots them to their respective slots. Time Boxing then forces you to accomplish tasks within limited periods thus imposing mini-deadlines and resolving many issues including perfectionism. If you decide you will spend 2 hours writing a letter, this reduces the time you'll spend editing and re-writing the letter after it is "good enough."

When compartmentalizing, Sonia also respects her energy patterns to maximize her effectiveness during each period of the day.

CLARIFY YOUR INTENTION

If you procrastinate because you can't decide what to tackle first, take a deep breath and turn your focus inward. Clarify your intention. Eliminate the distractions of emergencies and others' priorities. What results are you trying to achieve? Now ask, "What is the next step to take for this intention?" Let the answer come to you.

IF YOU PROCRASTINATE BECAUSE YOU CAN'T DECIDE WHAT TO TACKLE FIRST, TURN YOUR FOCUS INWARD.

This requires thinking time, which is probably on back order right now, but the less thinking time you have, the busier you become. If you feel you're chasing your tail, you need to invest some time clarifying your objectives, selecting your most important project and deciding where to focus your time and energy.

When Sonia books some quiet "thinking time" to clarify her intention, she realizes she has been in execution mode. As she explains, when she doesn't review her objectives regularly to clarify what she needs to do to make them happen, she "loses her way." Seeing that she needs to free up more time in her agenda for thinking, she hires a virtual assistant who could execute many of the day-to-day tasks she's been doing herself but that are preventing her from thinking strategically.

SELECT ONLY THREE TASKS

Selecting the tasks you'll work on and scheduling them in your agenda ahead of time will ease the pressure and free you from making mundane decisions each day. However, there's a catch. Don't overbook. Only select three tasks to focus on each day. Remember, most people cannot perform more than three to five significant tasks in a day, unless they are very short tasks such as phone calls.

PLANNING PROBLEMS ARE SURMOUNTABLE.

Planning problems are surmountable. Solutions include breaking projects into manageable chunks and practicing good self-management by using your agenda rather than your To-Do List to determine what you will do at any given time, respecting your energy patterns and scheduling time to think. You can also ask for help and use strategies such as externalizing your thoughts, compartmentalizing, clarifying your intentions and limiting your focus to three significant tasks daily.

CONQUERING PROCRASTINATION DUE TO LIMITING AND DISTORTED BELIEFS

Limiting or distorted beliefs and fears are some of the most daunting causes of procrastination. Even when you take all the right steps to move forward, distorted beliefs can stop you dead in your tracks.

LIMITING OR DISTORTED BELIEFS AND FEARS ARE SOME OF THE MOST DAUNTING CAUSES OF PROCRASTINATION.

You may feel you base your beliefs on reality, but more commonly, people's beliefs result from a distorted interpretation of reality. For example, many people fear public speaking more than they fear dying. Obviously, they believe being embarrassed is a fate worse than death and just as obviously, this is not true. This is a distorted interpretation of reality but it affects people's behavior as effectively as, or even more than, reality.

If you are a salesperson, but you believe all salespeople are out to take care of their own needs at the expense of their clients, you are likely to sabotage any potential sale if taking advantage of others goes against your values.

If you believe all business people are crooks, you will struggle as an entrepreneur, unless, of course, you want to be a crook.

Limiting or distorted beliefs usually originate from your past, your family, your experiences, your culture, your peers or your friends. When faced with traumatic yet sometimes banal events in your past, you attempt to create meaning around them. The result is an interpretation, usually a faulty one, of what really happened. This interpretation leads you to adopt a distorted belief that guides you in avoiding a repetition of that event. These distortions become the foundation for your decisions and choices about everything.

As a child, I was interested in dance and often asked my parents for ballet lessons. The answer was "no, we can't afford it." I accepted this until my parents somehow found the funds to enroll my three brothers in a hockey league and purchased their hockey equipment. I figured we must have hit the mother lode and that now my parents were in a better position to afford ballet lessons for me. When again they answered that they couldn't afford it, I took it to mean that I was not a good enough investment of their money and carried this pain for a long time. This belief that "I wasn't enough" stopped me from thriving in my business because "I wasn't enough" to invest my family's money into my business, "I wasn't enough" to contact possible partners or collaborators. Why would they even want to talk to me? It has helped me tremendously to realize that "I wasn't enough" was a story I created to explain why my parents had never been willing to invest in me.

They aren't bad parents. They didn't have much money and chose to invest in hockey because they worried that my brothers could easily slip into a life of drugs or gangs and felt that involvement in sports would prevent that. In other words, they had confidence in me and felt I usually made good decisions for myself. This is quite a different reason than my interpretation.

> YOUR BELIEFS MAY HAVE SERVED YOU WELL ONCE UPON A TIME, BUT AS YOUR NEEDS CHANGE, MANY OF THESE BELIEFS LOSE THEIR RELEVANCE AND ACTUALLY IMPEDE YOUR PROGRESS.

You will feel uncomfortable attempting to do something that goes against your beliefs. To "protect" you, your subconscious will sabotage any attempt to complete the task. Your only solution is to question and change your beliefs, but this can be difficult, especially if you're not aware of the beliefs that keep you struck.

Your beliefs may have served you well once upon a time, but as your needs change, many of these beliefs lose their relevance and actually impede your progress.

Limiting or distorted beliefs manifest themselves in various ways such as perfectionism, fear, resistance and sabotage.

PERFECTIONISM

Sonia's perfectionism manifests as a decision-making problem because she struggles to make the perfect decision. However, Sonia's perfectionism, and all perfectionism, originates in faulty beliefs.

Sonia's perfectionism comes from her parent's insistence on "strong work ethics." Her parents often reprimanded her for not having paid attention to details. They didn't do it to be mean, they felt that careless mistakes could negatively affect her chances of success. Paradoxically, her excess care to avoid mistakes was doing exactly what her parents had been trying to avoid.

239

You might think perfectionism would be a desirable trait, but it is a productivity killer, not to mention being an impossible goal. Non-conformists, Creative Geniuses often deal with more than their fair share of reprimand, embarrassment or shame. Pegged as a dreamer, you may have been the brunt of jokes or ridiculed for your beliefs and mistakes. For Creative Geniuses diagnosed with ADHD, failure or difficulty in school, lost jobs and failed relationships add to an extreme desire to avoid failure.

FEAR

Fear is a common limiting belief. It's normal and sometimes desirable to be afraid; when you're standing on the ledge of a building, the fear of falling comes in handy. However, most fears are unreasonable.

MOST FEARS ARE UNREASONABLE.

Fear can paralyze you if you anticipate a negative outcome, or even if you think you might succeed, but that there is a chance you might fail. You may believe that if you fail, you won't be able to handle the consequences. Covering how to overcome fears could (and does) fill many books, but here we'll concentrate on those that frequently cause procrastination: the fear of failure and the fear of success.

FEAR OF FAILURE OR REJECTION

Fear of failure or of rejection is difficult to overcome; when you try something new, there is a real chance you might fail. However, we often give too much weight to failure as a possible outcome. If a car were likely to hit you if you crossed the street, it makes sense not to do it. However, if there is only a small chance that it could happen, it is unreasonable to feel paralyzed.

Failure is not binary; not everything that is not success is failure. When trying something new, the possible outcomes are success, failure and something in between. If you think that anything less than success is failure, or if you think the most likely outcome is failure, it's difficult to jump in and take a chance. However, if you reframe your belief so that anything other than outright failure is a degree of success, or that even failure is a learning experience, you're more likely to take considered risks.

You'll also feel paralyzed despite recognizing that your chances of success are good if you don't believe you can handle anything other than success. Past failures, and we all have them, serve as proof that mistakes sometimes lead to failure and can have negative consequences.

Patrick suffers from paralyzing fear. As an artist, he struggles to talk about his art, thinking he is terrible at communicating with others. He feels he tends to say the wrong things and to make others feel uncomfortable. Patrick is also afraid to sell his art. While he can create lots of art, fear paralyzes him when it comes to approaching galleries and agents.

Of course, as a Creative Genius you often must convince people to believe in, buy into or buy something that is a part of who you are, as is the case with Patrick's art. You must face the real possibility that some people won't like it. Patrick feels he would be unable to handle rejection so he rarely exposes his paintings.

FEAR OF SUCCESS

You might wonder how someone could be afraid of success. Isn't that what we all want? Of course, you desire success, but you might feel the side effects of success will be difficult to live with. You may doubt you can or would want to live up to what you anticipate will be expected of you. Success may even go against your beliefs.

Growing up, Patrick had been taught that real artists are "starving," sacrificing wealth for their art. After starting a Meet-Up group for artists, he also worries he won't fit in with his artist friends if he becomes successful. In a way, he fears success would lead to rejection by his peers.

He also thinks success means he'll probably have to talk to people, which he feels he is unable to do. He also worries that if "the impossible" happened and he found a gallery to represent him, he'd lose control of the direction of his art.

These conflicting beliefs create a lot of anxiety in Patrick so he retreats to his comfort zone, a place where all he needs to do is paint and enjoy art. His beliefs were keeping him from living his real dream, becoming a full-time artist.

Success also often brings with it increasing responsibilities. Sonia realizes she is afraid of success, even if she wants it as badly. She feels she can barely manage her current workload. If she had more contracts, she'd have more to do, which she doesn't think she can handle. Realizing she has this fear helps Sonia explain why she has been struggling to prepare proposals; not only does she hates doing them, the results don't inspire her much because she fears she can't handle more on her plate.

SOLUTIONS TO YOUR LIMITING BELIEFS

You aren't a prisoner of your limiting or distorted beliefs. Becoming aware of the source of the belief can help you resolve it, by allowing you to separate what really happened from the interpretation you gave it. However, at other times its source is so deeply repressed, you may only be able to gain awareness of the belief itself but not of where it originated.

YOU AREN'T A PRISONER OF YOUR LIMITING OR DISTORTED BELIEFS.

Awareness of a belief is enough and plays a big part in resolving it. As you become aware of the belief that's holding you back, you can then question its validity and correct it.

Regardless of your belief, you are not stuck with it. You always have the choice to believe otherwise. Conquering procrastination due to your limiting or distorted beliefs requires that you overcome and change your limiting beliefs, essentially attacking the problem at the source.

SHIFT YOUR BELIEFS

The steps to overcome and change your limiting beliefs are:

1. Become aware of your belief.
2. Question and examine its validity.
3. Decide who you want to be: are you someone who is limited by your beliefs or someone who is empowered by them?
4. Shift and restate your belief so that it supports who you want to be, someone who's empowered by your beliefs.
5. Take steps immediately to prove your new belief is the right one.
6. When fear creeps up again (this is normal), clarify your vision of who you want to be and where you want to go and then revisit the process.

Let's examine Patrick's belief that he can't talk to people. Once he becomes aware of his fear of rejection, he examines the validity of his assumption through journaling.

At first, he is able to pinpoint numerous times when he'd said something that made a situation worse or made enemies. However, he also realizes that he's had a lot of success and acceptance when he spoke up in the past. He somehow attracted his wife, who is still in love with him, he's gotten numerous jobs after successful interviews and he even had a career as a very successful teacher that obviously demonstrated some communication skills. Faced with this evidence, he realizes his belief was simply not valid.

Next, in his journal he describes the type of person he wants to be: a successful artist, someone who believes in his art and someone who can handle rejection. He realizes he will never see eye to eye with everyone, and not everyone will like his art; however, he doesn't need everyone to like his art or to agree with everyone in order to be a successful artist. He just needs to please a small segment of the population, and that certainly seems possible.

Armed with new beliefs that 1) he could talk to people without making them dislike him; and 2) he could handle the possibility that some people won't like him or his art, he prepares a few questions to ask people when he first meets them and an "elevator speech," a 30-second introduction of himself as an artist. He practices it until he is comfortable with it and then tries it on a few people. The result, to his great surprise and pleasure, is that many of them want to know more about his art. To anchor this success, I encourage him to keep a Success Journal as a way to strengthen his belief that he is a capable conversationalist.

When examining the validity of your belief, ask yourself "What are the possible outcomes of doing what I'm afraid of?" As mentioned earlier, the answer is success, failure or something in between. If you choose to view failure and the "something in between" as learning experiences, you'll realize that even if things don't work out as planned, you're much further ahead.

Consider the odds of failure. How probable is it that you will fail? When Patrick weighed the evidence, he realized it was only on rare occasions that he'd "failed" when talking to people. Despite his newfound courage, every now and then, a moment of "failure" had him retreating to his comfort zone. Reviewing his dream and his Success Journal helped stop him from being a victim and to become a victor.

BELIEVE YOU CAN OVERCOME ANY SETBACKS

If you believe you're incapable of accomplishing a task, you will be right; because you'll feel there's no use trying. If you believe you are capable, you will be right; because you'll feel you'll be able to accomplish the task. Reality may prevent you from accomplishing certain things, but reality is not what's holding most people back. Rather, it's their limiting beliefs.

As a Creative Genius, you love ambitious projects and trying things you've never done before. It's natural that you'll face failures or setbacks from time to time. However, you <u>will</u> be able to overcome any setback. You are a resourceful, creative and capable person who can overcome any obstacle.

YOU ARE A RESOURCEFUL, CREATIVE AND CAPABLE PERSON WHO CAN OVERCOME ANY OBSTACLE.

Each failure or setback is simply a learning experience to help you figure out how to overcome the obstacles between you and your dreams.

As you can see, one of the most effective ways of dealing with procrastination is to dig down to the underlying limiting belief.

EACH FAILURE OR SETBACK IS SIMPLY A LEARNING EXPERIENCE TO HELP YOU FIGURE OUT HOW TO OVERCOME THE OBSTACLES BETWEEN YOU AND YOUR DREAMS.

Through questioning and brainstorming, Sonia comes up with a plan for how she could manage more success by hiring an administrative assistant and eventually a business manager, by creating systems to streamline her business and by delegating tasks to others.

CONQUERING PERFECTIONISM

When perfectionism hits, re-evaluate what success means for your project. The problem usually occurs when you "take your eyes off the prize" and focus your energies on the wrong definition of success. Thus, re-evaluating your success criteria is always the first critical step to overcoming perfectionism.

The second step is to identify what's creating the problem. Perfectionism results when you set your standards too high and you worry about backlash if you don't meet those standards.

Many Creative Geniuses secretly suspect other people do things better, faster and more systematically than they do. This is a distorted belief. When you try to measure up to your distorted perceptions of others' capabilities, you fail because your standards are unrealistic.

DEFINE SUCCESS

Unless you're building a high-rise, an automobile or an airplane, or you are a heart or brain surgeon, "100%" usually only needs to be about 80% of perfection. Let me illustrate.

There is always room for improvement, but unless these improvements give you a good return on investment, don't waste time on them. Don't neglect the "halo effect," which states that something pretty is more valued than something ugly; however, if it's accurate and "pretty good" then it's likely good enough.

How do your standards compare to your expectations of others? If you find it difficult to answer that question, ask someone else to help you gauge what is reasonable to expect in a given situation. You'll probably be surprised that they find what you consider passable more than good enough. Ask yourself:

✦ What is a successful outcome from completing the task you're procrastinating?

✦ What is the most important thing required for this successful outcome to occur?

For Sonia, a successful outcome from a proposal is to get the contract. What is the most important thing required for her to get the contract? Her answer? It's getting the proposal in the hands of her client on time.

STRIVE FOR EXCELLENCE INSTEAD OF PERFECTION

If you're not sure what excellence looks like, stop when you've reached what you consider 80% perfect. Ask a friend or colleague to give you feedback. Ask them if they would consider the outcome "successful" based on the work in its current state? Sonia asks someone she knows from a networking group to read her proposal and give her feedback. Her colleague feels the proposal is perfect and would have given her the contract based on it.

Sonia is still not convinced, so I ask her to track the amount of time it takes her to write her next proposal from start to 80% perfection and then from 80% to what she estimates is 100% perfect. She is shocked that it takes as much time to move from 80% to 100% as it does to write the proposal from start to 80%.

She finally does a live test. She delivers a few proposals she considers to be 80% perfect and, to her surprise, finds that she still gets as many positive outcomes when she strives for excellence rather than for perfection. Actually, she lands more jobs because more clients get their proposals on time.

REDUCE MISTAKES

The following steps help you reduce mistakes:

✦ Relax and breathe deeply to get rid of any anxiety you feel.

- ✦ Create a checklist that outlines the success criteria for activity, as well as any secondary criteria you feel are important.
- ✦ Check spelling and grammar on all documents on your computer or get them proofread. Then let it go.
- ✦ If necessary, delegate the task to an expert. Even if you want to look it over afterwards, you'll be reviewing it with fresh eyes. You can find resources to help with this on www.craigslist.com and www.elance.com.

MORE TIPS TO CONQUER PERFECTIONISM

Accept imperfections in things that aren't important; consider your return on time invested. If you work for someone, ask him or her to clarify the criteria for success. Explain that you are a perfectionist (bosses don't see that as a bad thing) so you need his or her help in determining when the work is done. Ask for help making sure you deliver critical work on time.

If you're an entrepreneur, use time boxing; limit the time you'll devote to a particular task and stick to it. If this is difficult, hire a coach to help you with accountability.

If you make a mistake, fix it without wasting time berating yourself for it. If others notice the mistake first, own up to it, apologize if it has caused them an inconvenience and then find a solution. Remember, "failures" are learning experiences; focus on the lesson to avoid repeating a mistake in the future. Strive for excellence, not perfection.

STRIVE FOR EXCELLENCE, NOT PERFECTION.

When Sonia notices she's returning to her perfectionist habits, she allows herself a set time for final editing, sets a timer and stops as soon as the timer rings.

CONCLUSION

To conquer procrastination, you must be aware of the problem. This means you must ask the right questions to get to the source of the problem and then attack the source.

When lack of interest is the source problem, solutions include: 1) bartering, delegating or dropping the task, 2) looking for ways to inject interest, novelty, competition, intrigue and sometimes urgency, 3) use momentum or 4) use a body double.

To resolve decision-making problems that cause you to procrastinate, clarify the problem or the intended results first, prioritize based on the situation and limit your decisions using preprogrammed decisions such as routines, systems or processes.

You can conquer procrastination caused by planning problems by: 1) implementing good self-management practices, 2) determining if it's a project or task and breaking projects down, 3) externalizing your thoughts using mind mapping or asking someone to interview you or to act as a sounding board, 4) asking for help, 5) compartmentalizing high-level thinking and detail-oriented execution separately, and 6) clarifying your intention.

Finally, to overcome your limiting beliefs, you must be aware of the belief that is holding you back. Change your belief by examining it, shifting it, finding evidence that the new belief is more sound and anchoring it with success. When limiting beliefs are causing procrastination due to perfectionism, define your success criteria and strive for excellence instead of perfection.

When you attack the problem at the source instead of with band-aid solutions, you're more likely to win the fight on procrastination.

To conquer procrastination you need to identify and define what you are procrastinating

1. Identify and define what you are procrastinating

    a) Break up the activity into tasks
    b) Consider how you feel when faced with each task
    c) Consider how you feel about the end result

2. Identify the root cause

    a) Lack of interest
    b) Decision-making problem
    c) Planning problem
    d) Limiting or distorted belief

3. Address the problem at the source

    a) Solutions to lack of interest
       i) Inject interest, novelty, competition or urgency
       ii) Barter, delegate, drop or delay
       ii) Use momentum to get you started
       iv) Use a body double
    b) Solutions to decision-making problems
       i) Prioritize by deadline, level of interest, level of impact
       ii) Use pre-programmed decisions: routines, decision templates
       ii) Establish a clear process

  c) Solutions to planning problems

       i) Clarify responsibility

ii) Practice good time management

iii) Clarify the problem or intended results

iv) Consider is it a project or a task

v) Externalize your thoughts with mind mapping, talking it out, etc.

vi) Compartmentalize high-level vs. detail-level planning

vii) Select 3 tasks to focus on

✦ Solutions to limiting beliefs

- Shift your beliefs
- Believe you can overcome any setbacks
- Re-evaluation what success means
- Strive for excellence rather than perfection

If you feel you'd like to get into action right now to build your dream, visit Conquer Procrastination Now! at **www. ConquerProcrastinationNow.com.**

For additional information and support, visit Coach Linda Walker at **www.CoachLindaWalker.com.**

CHAPTER TWENTY-ONE

MANAGING EXPECTATIONS

CHANGES TO YOUR ROUTINES OFTEN AFFECT OTHERS

Most people will accept changes in your routines more easily if they understand the benefits. Generous people will go along with changes if they know it'll help you. Everyone else will go along with changes if they feel it will also benefit or not affect them. Developing new routines and patterns will help you get things done on time, prevent losing or forgetting things and eliminate many other mistakes or problems, many of which also affect other people.

Invest some time to point out how changes to your patterns and routines will solve or prevent those problems, and how that will benefit them. They'll quickly get with the program. Most people are far more interested in the result than they are in how you get there.

In this chapter, we'll look at how you can manage expectations and gain the support of the people around you on your quest to reach your full potential.

INVEST TIME TO POINT OUT THE BENEFITS OF CHANGING TO YOUR PATTERNS AND ROUTINES.

After learning how routines could improve his productivity, John decides to make some changes at work. However, he soon feels the brunt of his colleagues' dissatisfaction. John wisely chooses to answer emails at a set time in the early afternoon instead of letting every incoming email disrupt his work. His teammates, used to an immediate response to any email they send him, interpret this lack of urgency as complacency and complain to his boss. When John explains the reasons behind this change in his routine, and demonstrates the increase in productivity he has achieved in a very short time, his boss is better able to support him.

John could have prevented this entire episode by announcing his intentions in a team meeting prior to making the change. All problems are resolved when John finally announces, "I know many of you are waiting on me to get on with your next task. I work best in the morning, but I've been struggling to get things done because I use that time to read my email, and interrupt my work to respond every time one arrives. To prevent holding you up, I've decided to turn off my email until just before lunch. I'll handle anything that comes up first thing in the afternoon, but of course, in a real emergency, just come see me. That way, I'll be much more productive and I'll be able to deliver the things you're waiting on."

He also prepares a voice message in which he explains to callers why he isn't available (I'm working on your projects) and when he'll return their calls (after lunch and at the end of the day).

Managing expectations is essential when you're implementing any change, and omitting this step can derail your best intentions.

Sonia knows changes in her hours of operation will affect her clients, so she manages expectations by adding a policy stating her contact hours in the contracts clients sign with her before any project starts.

To ensure her clients have read and are aware of this, Sonia makes sure that she explains her hours to her clients and reminds them when they'll talk. She is surprised when most clients seem fine with her work hours and respect them. She had anticipated some clients would be mad and refuse to sign with her, but that has not happened. Sonia is asserting her boundaries in a non-threatening way and making sure her clients are clear about them early in the relationship.

Patrick plans to change when he'll schedule his writing projects. Unfortunately, his supervisor often assigns writing projects in the afternoon when he is not effective for projects requiring concentration. He discusses with his supervisor that he will schedule his writing projects in the morning because he is better able to concentrate, and explains that writing projects assigned to him in the afternoon would only be treated the next morning. Patrick uses afternoons to manage emails, make phone calls and do research. She is impressed with his level of organization and by his initiative. She is also impressed with his resulting productivity improvement.

Patrick also speaks to his wife and children about the changes in his agenda when he decides to dedicate Monday and Wednesday evenings and Saturday morning to his art. He also asks their help to prepare the menu and grocery list for the next week. He negotiates Thursday as a good evening for all of them to spend 20 minutes preparing the list.

Finally, he asks for their support when he sometimes reverts to his old habit of watching TV and surfing the Web on nights when he had planned to paint. He asks his wife to question him when he is not working as scheduled. In addition, his family makes sure not to ask him to engage in other activities on days he has put aside for working on his art.

When managing expectations, it's important to identify those affected by your changes and to make a plan to communicate the change. You can also solicit their support as a way to keep you on the straight and narrow.

Consider communicating the following:

+ What the change will be
+ Why you are implementing this change
+ How the change will affect them
+ What's in it for them (AKA, the benefits)
+ You are available to discuss any concerns
+ Ask for their support

Communication is an important part of change. If you don't ensure your environment is ready to support you, you're more likely to abandon your new habit, system or other change. Manage expectations so that others around you are aware of what you're changing, how it will and you and how they can support you.

COMMUNICATION IS AN IMPORTANT PART OF CHANGE.

One major benefit John finds in managing his agenda better is that it is easier for him to provide his colleagues and clients with shorter turnaround and better quality work for them. You'll probably find, as Sonia, Patrick and John did, that when people are aware of what's coming they tend to be supportive.

CONCLUSION

When you attack the problem at its source rather than applying band-aid solutions, and you advise people about coming changes, you're far more likely to be successful, whatever goals you're reaching for.

- ✦ Most people accept change to your routines if they understand the benefit

- ✦ Invest some time to point out how changes in your patterns will solve or prevent problems

- ✦ Most people want results and are not interested in how you got there

- ✦ Communicate

  - What the change will be
  - Why you are implementing it
  - How the change will affect them
  - Help them see the benefits
  - Communicate your openness to discussion
  - Ask for support

For additional information and support, visit Coach Linda Walker at **www.CoachLindaWalker.com.**

If you feel you'd like to get into action right now to radically change your life and tap into your assets, visit The Maximum Productivity Makeover at **www. MaximumProductivityMakeover.com.**

PART SIX. PAVE THE WAY FOR CHANGE – CONCLUSION

P aving the way for change demands that you eliminate obstacles to peak performance. One of the most devastating obstacles we face is procrastination but perfectionism, fear of failure (and fear of success) play their parts as well. The good news is that in all cases, there are strategies to help you overcome these obstacles and improve your productivity. More good news is that there are also strategies you can use to enlist the help and support of the people around you by communicating the coming changes and managing expectations, an essential step that is often overlooked.

PART SEVEN

FINAL OUTCOMES

PART SEVEN. FINAL OUTCOMES

Creative Geniuses with big dreams who embrace who they are, and who believe they are capable of even more than they have achieved to date, experience the greatest results.

The process we described in *With Time to Spare* is the one I use with my individual coaching clients as those enrolled in the group coaching program, *The Maximum Productivity Makeover for Creative Geniuses,* which helps you accomplish more, more easily, despite the pressures of our crazy-busy world, all without stifling your amazing creativity. Yes, you must become aware of your weaknesses, but mainly so you can avoid them and focus on your strengths and interests. The objective of *The Maximum Productivity Makeover for Creative Geniuses* is to devise a plan to increase the time and energy you invest to use and develop your strengths and interests, while finding ways to keep weaknesses from derailing your plans.

Several years after we worked together, I contacted John to see how his self-management system was serving him. When I called John, I heard a pleasant greeting on his voicemail. I was grinning from ear to ear when John called me back; he apologized for not answering but explained that I had called during his Focus Time and he always let the voicemail pick up during that time.

He mentioned that initially he had struggled to change his habits and he would sometimes fall back into his old habits, but each time he found his life spinning out of control, re-applying the *Creative Genius Maximum Productivity* principles would get him quickly back on track, so he stuck with them and before long, he'd solidified these new habits. He said his life has been going amazingly well ever since.

He fulfils his commitments with his children, friends and colleagues on time every time. His colleagues and bosses notice and appreciate the shorter delivery times. He explains that in the past, he'd overstate his estimated delivery date by as much as two to three months because he never knew if he'd be able to get to them.

He uses his agenda diligently and after three years, he still guards his peak performance time. He exercises regularly, uses an automated savings system. He mentions his astonishment that while in the past, he'd work until 10 or 11 pm every day, now, at 4:30 pm he is consistently done for the day and feels free to leave without guilt, in fact, he feels satisfied with what he accomplishes each day.

His satisfaction stems from delivering all his projects ahead of deadlines, being an asset to his colleagues and more importantly, the resulting feeling of self-confidence and competence he's developed.

He's also happy he now knows how to help his sons, both of whom are Creative Geniuses with ADHD. He's able to be a good role model for them. He tells me that while change was difficult and took longer than he would have liked, he succeeded by doing it one step at a time and it has definitely been worth it.

Patrick recently had his first solo exhibit, has been accepted in his first gallery and is selling his art. In addition, his newfound ability to talk to others with confidence has allowed him to make several excellent contacts leading to radio and TV interviews. He is pursuing more excellent leads to sell ever more of his art, and while his art is not bringing in enough revenue for him to leave his job yet, he no longer feels trapped. He's been able to increase his productivity so much that he can do his job, paint 20 hours a week and help at home, all without losing control of his life. He's exercising, has lost a lot of weight and watches very little television, opting instead to paint or draw, which is much more fulfilling for him. He's involved with a group of artists who support each other in their careers. He's even accumulating savings in preparation for leaving his job, and his finances are in order because he's incorporated time in his busy schedule to pay his bills.

His relationship with his wife has greatly improved; she now feels she has a partner she can rely on to share the challenges of running a home and organizing family life. He mentions that since his system has been in place, he finds it has become easy to follow and, in fact, he says it's become such an ingrained habit that it would be more difficult not to follow it. He reviews his objectives regularly and is on track to realize his big dreams, which compels him to stretch out of his comfort zone. He tells me with a big smile, "Life is good."

Entrepreneurs are really Creative Geniuses who happen to express their creativity by creating their own business. As I mentioned, Sonia is an aggregate of many of my entrepreneurial clients. When entrepreneurs come to me, often many aspects of their lives are going well because they already focus on their strengths and have the freedom to adjust their work schedule and environment to their unique needs. They usually consult me for advice and strategies to solve problems in a few key areas of their lives.

When we work together, my entrepreneurial clients usually build a team to help them manage paperwork and make sure invoices, proposals and contracts go out on time. We streamline their processes and systems, especially processes involving their clients, from how they approach new prospects to how they offer their services and from the contracting process all the way to final payment. Whenever possible, we automate their processes, making them more easy to delegate. As an extra benefit, this adds value to the business should they decide to sell it (many Creative Genius entrepreneurs sell their businesses when they get bored, preferring the thrill of building a new business from the ground up to the stability of managing a successful company.)

Delegating the minutia of business life to systems, processes and to employees makes them feel more in control of their business, their finances and their lives. They also feel more confident in their decisions as they have established clear processes for making them. Most importantly, they have more time to take advantage of their strengths. They have more time to think, leading to better focus and clarity. They are able to exercise, get more rest and stay healthy. And even though they are doing more, they feel less overwhelmed by their workload. They are more involved in their family and even have time to pursue other interests.

Creative Genius entrepreneurs thrive on excitement as they grow their business, win new clients and launch new products. However, the growth in most businesses eventually stabilizes, fewer new products are offered, and capturing new clients becomes too easy.

Creative Genius entrepreneurs need an exit strategy because when they become bored with their business, they grow distracted and lose their way, or in some cases, they subconsciously sabotage their businesses in order to create an exciting situation (problem) they can solve.

As a coach, I choose to work with Creative Geniuses like yourself because I believe you hold the best hope for solving the world's most pressing problems. Among your brilliant ideas, you may have already discovered an out-of-the-box approach that will help eliminate poverty, global warming, hunger or pollution. You may have found a better way to do something or invented a new gadget that will bring value to people. Or you may have some humanitarian work that you'd like to pursue. No matter what ambitious goals you may have, given your tremendous strengths, all you need is a way to take care of your life without stifling your amazing creativity or wasting your talents and strengths and success will come. Every day, I feel privileged to work with people just like you, empowering you to do your best work and live your best life.

My hope is that this book has inspired and empowered you to do just that.

To your Focus Action Success,

Linda

For additional information and support, visit Coach Linda Walker at **www.CoachLindaWalker.com.**

If you feel you'd like to get into action right now to radically change your life and tap into your assets, visit The Maximum Productivity Makeover at **www.MaximumProductivityMakeover.com.**

AFTERWORD

I hope you enjoyed With Time To Spare and you are already starting to take action in applying some of the strategies described in this book.

In my many years as coach, I have met many people who are in search of information to help them manage their lives. They gobble every book and course they can. They read and even keep every article ever on subjects that interest them. They may even spend huge amounts of time talking about their findings, spreading the word about what they've read in a way allowing them to be heroes.

All of this activity around learning and still they feel frustrated. Nothing worked for them. The problem is that they missed one particularly important step, implementing what they've learned.

If you find yourself in this group, I acknowledge for your appetite for learning and your persistence at find the book or course that will allow you to Be Who You really believe yourself to be. And now, I encourage you to take the next step and implement in your own life one strategy you've learned. Start right now!

If you feel overwhelmed or you'd like to be accompanied in this journey, I invite you to find a coach who resonates with you. It could be me or someone else, just find him or her and start moving forward in your life.

To your Focus Action Success!

Linda Walker

How to find us: www.CoachLindaWalker.com

INDEX

A

abnormal sleep patterns, 110
accepting a new assignment
    questions to ask, 232
accountability, 248
act as if, 61–62
action time, 110–11
    definition, 108
    physical activity, 110
addiction
    to television, 14
    to the Web, 14
    to video games, 14
ADHD, i–iii, v, 18, 27
    and addictions, 14
    and big picture thinking, 12
    and boredom, 117–18
    and failure, 240
    and focus, 134
    and goal setting, 49
    and heredity, 27
    and idea generation, 12–13
    and interest, 117–18
    and organizing, 222
    and planning, 222
    and prioritizing, 222
    and problem solving, 12–13
    and structure, 173
    and tardiness, vi
    and television, 14
    and time management,
    185–86
    and video games, 14

difference, 9–15
effect on marriage, 173
getting work done, 221
living with, i
managing, ii
overcoming boredom,
220–21
symptoms, v–vii
adrenaline, 224
adrenaline junkies, 14
agenda, 175, 202–5
    characteristics of, 175–79
    commitments, 175–77
    electronic, 175
    habit of using, 81
    managing your, 202–5
    multiple, 177
    paper-based, 176
    portability, 177
    preparing meeting agenda,
    141
    the right, 175–79
    uses, 176–77
agenda vs. to-do list, 237
alerts, 190–91
announcing change, 254
annual planning, 195, 196–97
Anthony Robbins, 98
anticipating interruptions, 223
ask for help, 234
assignments
    before accepting, 232
Attention Deficit Hyperactivity

Disorder. *See* ADHD

attention span. *See* concentration

avoiding

effectiveness of, 151

avoiding overbooking, 236

awareness of belief, 243

B

bad habit. *See* habits

bad moods, 150

bartering, 188, 217

belief

    self, 32

beliefs, 28–32

    be aware of, 29–30

    causes of, 237–42

    distorted, 242

    empowering, 31

    interpretation, 237

    limiting, 237–42, 242–46

    overcoming limiting, 29–32

    serving you, 239

best meeting practices, 141

big picture, 235

big picture focus, 230

BNI, 149

body double, 221

boredom

    and ADHD, 215, 217

boring tasks, 215

    making them fun, 219–20

boundaries, 255

    establish, 132

limiting availabilities, 131–32

    setting effective, 131–36

brain

    and ADHD, 220

breaking down tasks, 214

C

calendars. *See* also agenda

    characteristics of, 175–79

    multiple, 173, 177

    uses, 176–77

celebrate accomplishments, 196-97

    creating habit of, 97

Chamber of Commerce, 149

change, 47

    and learning, 69

    communicating, 254, 256

    managing, 45–49, 253–56

    patterns, 253

    resistance to, 23, 45

    routines, 253

change process, 45–49

checking agenda

    habit, 191

checklist, 248

    systems, 86

choices, 150

chunking, 237

chunking tasks, 214

clarifying expectations, 231

clarifying objectives, 236

clarifying responsibilities, 231

clutter
    and beliefs, 144
    psychological aspects, 144–45
    stop, 146
    stress-inducing and
    distracting, 144
    cost of, 143
coach, 248
cognitive hyperactivity, 110
comfort zone, 45, 46, 66, 242
    out of your, 204–5
commit to others
    creating habits, 97
commitment tools, 202–5
commitments, 2, 6, 195
    and self-esteem, 28
    effect of broken, 173
    honor, 201
    remembering, 201
    schedule, 176
communicating change, 256
communication, 133
    and boundaries, 132, 136
    and procrastination, 128
    better, 151–52
    managing, 131–33
    to manage change,
    253–56
compartmentalizing, 235
concentration, iv, 108
    fluctuations in, 108
    improving, 108–10, 117–21
    inability to, v

conflict, 152
conquer procrastination, 211–51
conquering boredom
    systems, 81
control your productivity, 176
correct
    limiting beliefs, 243
create meaning, 238
creative genius, v–vii
    and distractions, 220
    characteristics of, 20
    defined, 9–15
creativity
    and systems, 81
criteria for success, 229
cubicle farms
    interruptions, 133
culture
    cause of distorted beliefs,
    238

D

daydreaming
    obstacles to productivity, 129
deadlines, 202
    missed, 174
decision template, 226–27
decision-making
    limiting, 225
    problems with, 221–23
    rules to simplify, 227
    set a time limit, 227
    simplifying, 226–27

solutions to, 188,
224–28
decisions
preprogrammed, 225–28
decluttering, 143–45
definition, 137
defining success, 246–47
delegating, 161–63, 188, 218–19
to systems, 225
details
focus on, 230
disorganization, iv, 7, 144–45
distorted beliefs, 237–42
distraction, v, vi, 7, 13, 20
and boredom, 221
and clutter, 143
and communications, 128–30
and ideas, 138
and urgency, 229
and work environment, 18
eliminate, 235
interruptions, 138–39
doing it yourself
alternatives to, 163
cost of, 161–63, 165
dream, 57–60
and goal setting, 24–28
building, 61
drop in
interruption, 132
drop-off area
for keys, sunglasses, PDA,
cell phone, bus pass, 143

E

electronic agenda, 175
alert advantage, 190
email
clutter, 154–55
for group decisions, 141
instead of meeting, 141
interruption, 128
managing, 131–33
response, 254
system, 86
time traps, 157
emotional brain, 47
emotional control
signs of loss of energy, 114
empathy
to stop rumination, 152
empowering belief, 31
energy
decreased, 105–15
drop, 105–15
high physical, 110–11
energy fluctuations
schedule around, 106
energy levels, 202
and planning, 202
energy patterns, 108–10
and task characteristics, 123
environment
support, 64
estimating time, 185–87
to complete tasks, 201–2
excellence vs. perfectionism, 247

exercise, 6, 81, 129
  and habits, 96
  planning systems, 202
  starting a program, 71–73
  systems to, 86, 186
expectations
  managing, 254
experiences
  and distorted beliefs, 238
external calls to action
  creating habits, 96

F

failure
  as a learning experience,
  196-197, 240
  fear of, 240–41
faith, 59
family
  cause of distorted beliefs,
  238
  environment, 64
fear
  of embarrassment, 237
  of success, 241–42
  procrastination due to,
  240–42
  public speaking, 237
  solutions to, 242–46
feeling of anxiety, 114
fidgetiness, 114
fighting
  solutions to, 151

filter to-do list
  planning process, 199–203
firefighter mode, 224
floaters, 190
  in time management system,
  190
focus, 3, 108, 139 *See*
concentration
  improving, 117–21
  shifting, 229–30
focus time, 108–10
  definition, 108
food shopping
  system, 86
free time
  lack of, 153–54
friends
  cause of distorted beliefs,
  238

G

Gallup Organization, 34
get motivated, 57–60
getting organized
  and resources, 143
Getting Things Done, 185
goals, 44
  and emotions, 26, 60–62
  challenging, 26
  setting, 48–54, 197
gratitude, 62
grocery shopping
  system for, 218

gym
    system for exercising, 86

H
habits, 91–99, 100, 191
    alarms, 95
    and achieving goals, 91, 93
    and clutter prevention, 144
    and decision making, 93
    and exercise, 96
    and needs, 92
    and planning, 195
    and productivity, 225
    and success, 87, 93
    bad, 99, 129, 149–55
    breaking bad, 91, 92, 95, 97, 149
    building new, 94–98
    common bad, 153–56
    conserve energy, 93
    creating new, 92
    daily routine, 95
    develop, 14
    dream building, 95
    for agenda, 191
    increase your motivation, 96–97
    maintenance, 94
    make it easier, 97–98
    resistance to change, 97
    save time and energy, 93
    saving, 96
    spending, 38

    support to break, 255
    to limit decisions, 225–28
    triggers, 94
    what to make into, 94
halo effect, 246
handbag, 143
high standards, 246
high stress, 110
homeless shelter
    definition, 144
honoring commitments, 201, 203
hours of operation, 254
How to Mind Map, 234
hyperfocus, 11–12, 108
    attaining, 108–10

I
idea journal, 139, 145
ideas
    and ADHD, 12–13
imperfections
    accepting, 248
importance
    definition, 224
improving efficiency
    streamline, 92
improving focus, 108–10
improving productivity, 108–10
    energy fluctuations, 105
impulsivity, 30
    and productivity, 138
in control of your life, 204

in the zone
hyperfocus, 108
inability to concentrate
signs of loss of energy, 114
increasing productivity
by recharging, 113
information addiction,
154–55
instant gratification, 23
intention
clarifying, 235–36
interactive alerts, 190–91
interest, 189, 219
and ADHD, 117–18, 215,
219–20
and procrastination,
216–21
eliminate boredom,
219–20
level of, 117
internal language
and mood, 150–51
interruption log, 134, 138
interruptions, 128
preventing, 223
intuition
and ADHD, 12–13
John
introduction to, 18–19

K
Kurt Lewin, 46

L
lack of clarity
and procratination, 229
lack of interest
causes of procrastination,
216–21
lack of motivation, 66
language
internal, 150–51
late
cost of being, 143
working, 18, 19
layered learning, 69–75
definition of, 69
steps to, 72
learning
from failure, 196–97
from success, 196–97
layered, 69–75
overcome procrastination,
69–72
life vision, 27–28
limiting beliefs, 237–42
overcome, 242–46
list
personal development, 189
project task, 179–83
routine task, 188–89
stop-doing, 187–88
strengths, 189
to manage life, 175
losing control
of success, 242

losing temper
   avoid, 151
lost time
   making up for, 19

M

managing appointments, 175
managing expectations
   script for, 254
managing paperwork, 164
managing projects, 198, 199
managing time, 173–206
maximizing productivity and
creativity, 109
maximum productivity, 106
media
   clutter, 154–55
meditation, 112
meeting planning, 140
meeting practices
   clear roles for each attendee,
   141
   reduce meeting times,
   142
meeting your needs, 92
meetings
   alternatives to, 141
   more efficient, 140
Meetup, 65
mental energy, 108
   energy fluctuations, 106
milestones, 181
   definition, 233

mind mapping
   externalizing thoughts, 234
missed deadlines, 174
mistakes
   as a learning experience, 240
   correcting, 248
   reducing, 247–48
momentum
   and ADHD, 220–21
monthly planning, 197–98
mood
   and communication, 151–52
   improve, 151–52
   manage your, 150–52
motivated
   becoming, 24–28
   getting, 57–67
   staying, 24–28, 62–64
motivation, 24–28, 57–67
   find, 57–60
   keep your, 62–64
music
   and motivation, 63

N

naps, 112
needs
   meeting your, 37–39
   unmet, 37–39
neurotypicals
   definition, 9
next year
   planning, 196–97

no time, 153–54

noise-reducing headphones, 135

non-conformity

    resisting systems, 82

not good enough, 238

not-to-do list, 157–60, 175, 187

    definition of, 157

    planning process, 200

    what to do with, 158

O

objectives

    clarifying, 236

obstacles

    overcome, 62–64

    to free time, 153–56

    to productivity, 128–30, 211

old habits

    breaking, 92

open-door policies

    interruptions, 128, 133

opportunity cost, 162

organization, 234

    of meeting, 140–42

    physical, 143–44

    poor, 129

organize

    struggle to, 184

organized, 6

    financial incentive to being, 143

    get and stay, vi

    struggle to get, 137

struggle to stay, 58

organizing your thoughts

    difficulty with, 228

    mind mapping, 234

over commitment, 155

over-active mind, 110

overbooking

    eliminate, 176, 236

overcoming

    boredom, 220–21

    perfectionism, 69–72, 235

    procrastination, 69–72

    resistance to planning, 203–4

    setbacks, 245–46

    weaknesses, 200–201

overcommitment, 13–14, 149–50, 149

    solution, 150

overwhelm, iv, 13, 149, 222

    caused by decision, 17, 221–23

    due to lack of recharge, 105–15

    procrastination, 229

    signs of loss of energy, 114

overwhelmed, vi

    by to-do list, 180

P

paper-based system, 176, 190

paperwork

    improve efficiency, 123

    managing, 164

    reduce the time, 123

passion, 59
past
    cause of distorted beliefs, 238
Patrick
    introduction to, 17–18
payoff of procrastination, 212
PDA, 176
    challenges, 177
    definition, 176
peak performance, 123
    best time to complete each
    task, 123
    self awareness, 139
peak productivity, 108–10, 112
peers
    cause of distorted beliefs, 238
perception
    and mood, 150–52
perfectionism
    and decision templates, 227
    conquer, 246–48
    faulty beliefs, 239–40
    overcome, 70, 246–48
    procrastinatiion due to, 223,
    246–48
    productivity killer, 240
    vs. excellence, 247
performance
    and productivity, 5
personal development list,
189
phone calls
    interruption, 128

physical activity, 119
    be more focused and less
    impulsive, 111
    task characteristic, 119
planning
    and energy patterns, 202
    annual, 196–97
    effective, 178
    for success, 195–206
    monthly, 197–98
    problems with, 228–31
    projects, 199
    quarterly, 196–97
    solutions to problems with,
    231–37
    time, 138, 198–206
    weekly, 198–206
planning process, 198–206
    and routines, 202
    checking not-to-do list, 200
    filter to-do list, 199–202
    overcome weaknesses,
    200–201
    strengths development,
    200–201
poor habits
    obstacles to productivity, 129
portability
    of self-management system,
    190
portable computerized agenda.
See PDA
post-it notes

floaters, 190
 in self-management, 190
preparation
 for activities, 186
priorities, 139
 set your own, 107
prioritizing, 49, 129, 139, 181,
182, 224–25
 and decision-making, 222
 based on
  impact, 224
  importance, 224
 by context, 185
 by level of importance, 184
 by level of interest, 185
 deadline, 224
 difficulty, 184
 problem with, 222
problem solving
 and ADHD, 12–13
process
 clarify the, 227
procrastination
 and communication, 128–30
 and energy, 59
 and long to-dos, 184
 and momentum, 163
 and self-management, 174
 and traditional approaches,
 212
 and values, 35
 benefits of, 212
 define what, 213–16

due to complicated task, 230
 due to lack of interest, 216–21
 due to planning problems,
 228–31
 lack of clarity, 229
 lack of knowledge, 229
 lack of ressources, 229
 overcoming, 211–51, 224–28
 solutions to, 217–21, 221
 steps to conquer, 213
procrastination solution, 231–37
 self-management, 231–32
productive
 vs. busy, 137–38
productivity, 2, 5–7
 and creativity, 5–7
 and energy levels, 105
 and energy patterns, 108–10
 and perfectionism, 240
 and structure, 82
 control your, 176
 definition of, 5–7
 improving, 20, 106, 108–10,
 117–21
 obstacles to, 128–30
project planning, 197–98
project task list, 175, 179–83
 how to create, 181–82
 organizing multiple, 183
 vs. to-do list, 180
projects
 systems for repetitive, 180
 vs. tasks, 184, 230, 233

purchases
and anxiety, 145
purse, 143

Q
quarterly planning, 195, 196–97
question beliefs, 239
questions
before accepting assignments, 232

R
recharge time, 105–15
definition, 108
improving productivity, 112
reducing mistakes
strategies for, 247–48
reducing stress
with frequent breaks, 113
rejection
fear of, 240–41
relationship
and fighting, 151
division of labour, 174
reminders, 190
top three priorities, 139
repetitive projects
systems for, 180
replenishing your energy, 112
resistance, 204–5
cost of, 170–71
to change, 23, 45, 57, 97, 210
to planning, 203–4

to scheduling, 232
responsibilities
clarifying, 231
for success, 242
return on investment, 246
reward yourself
creating habits, 96
right brain, 47
ROI, 246
routine activities
and planning, 202
to increase productivity, 111
routine task list, 175, 188–89, 188
routines
creating, 225–26
systems help accomplish goals, 83
to limit decisions, 225–28
RSS, 154–55
rumination, 152
definition of, 150
obstacles to productivity, 129

S
sabotage, 238, 239
scheduling
by area of work, 235
scheduling activities
commitments vs. energy patterns, 107
scheduling to improve productivity, 107

script, 150
    managing expectations, 134,
    254
    preparing for changes, 134
second wind
    recharge time, 113
self-control
    master, 204
self-esteem
    and honoring commitments,
    28
self-management
    definition of. *See* time
    management
    solution to procrastination,
    231–32
self-management system. *See*
time management system
    and procrastination, 212–13
    portability, 190
    traditional approaches,
    212–13
setbacks
    overcoming, 245–46
setting boundaries, 131–36
setting goals, 48–54, 197
    and positive psychology,
    51–52
setting intention, 235–36
shifting attention, 186, 229-30
shifting beliefs
    steps to, 243
shoulds, 58, 215

SMART goals, 45
    definition, 49–51
smart phones, 176
social media, 153
    obstacles to productivity, 129
social psychology, 46
solutions to planning problems
    clarify intended results,
    232–33
Sonia
    introduction to, 15–17
spontaneity
    fear of loss of, 173
stick with a plan
    energy fluctuations, 106
stop doing
    how to, 165
stop-doing list, 161–66, 175,
187–88
strengths, 33–35
    definition of, 33
    developing, 34–35
    identifying, 34
strengths development
    and planning, 200–201
stress, 6
structure, 173
    and creativity, 82
sub-project, 181
success
    afraid of, 241
    criteria, 246–47
    defining, 246–47

learning opportunities,
196–97
side effect of, 241
successful outcome
defining, 247
support groups, 65
supportive environment,
64–66
sustainable self-management,
203
systems, 81–89
benefit of, 81
definition, 82
enhancing creativity, 82
exercise, 86
food shopping, 86
for saving money, 85
how to create, 84
resistance to, 82–83
self-management, 31
time management, v
using templates, 85
when to use, 83

T

take control
of your productivity, 131
taking stock
of successes, 196–97
talents, 33–35
tardiness
and ADHD, vi
cost of, 16

task
allotting correct time, 201–2
characteristics, 117
concentration, 118
duration, 119, 201–2
interest, 214
planning, 117
significant completed per day,
139
vs. project, 184, 230, 233
telephone
managing, 131–33
telework, 140
temper, 151
templates, 218, 225
text message
interruptions, 128
The Artist's Way, 65
The Maximum Productivity
Makeover for Creative Geniuses,
10, 152
thinking time, 236
time
as an asset, 195
how much to allott, 185–87
time boxing, 235, 248
time estimating
for ADHD, 185–86
time for hobbies
finding, 153–54
time management, 173–206
myth about, 170
resistance to, 29

traditional approaches to, 9–10, 54–55, 54, 105, 107
time management system, v
    alerts, 190–91
    and beliefs, 31
    and personal development, 189
    floaters, 190
    integrated system, 189
    not-to-do list, 187
    routines, 188
    stop-doing list, 187
    to-do list, 183
time to think, 236
time to travel
    allotting, 186
time traps, 157–60, 187
timer, 220
Toastmasters, 66, 189
to-do list, 175, 198
    filtered, 203
    long, 184
    managing your, 183–87
    unrealistic, 139
    update, 199
    vs. problems with, 180
Tony Buzan's, 234
transition time, 119
transitions, 186
travel
    allotting time to, 186
TV, 153
    obstacles to productivity, 129

types of time
    focus, action and recharge, 108–14

U

unmet needs, 37–39
unreasonable expectations
interruptions, 133
untapped potential, 33–35
urgency, 220

V

validity
    of limiting beliefs, 243
values, 35–37
    honor your, 36–37
    identifying your, 35–36
video games, 153
    obstacles to productivity, 129
virtual assistant, 188
vision, 195
vision board, 63
voice message, 254
volunteering, 149–50, 149

W

watching TV, 153
weaknesses
    and planning, 200–201
    overcoming, 33
Web surfing
    obstacles to productivity, 129
weekly planning, 176, 198–206

where to start
    not knowing, 222
willpower, 57
    and motivation, 46–47
working backwards
    in defining project, 182
writing proposals, 214, 215, 216

RESOURCE GUIDE

We recommend the following resources to further explore the concepts provided in this book. We also recommend the references and resources already mentioned within the book text.

RECOMMENDED READING

ADD-Friendly Ways to Organize Your Life: Strategies that Work from a Professional Organizer and a Renowned ADD Clinician by Judith Kolberg and Kathleen Nadeau. New York, NY. Brunner Routledge. 2002

Delivered from Distraction: Getting the Most out of Life with Attention Deficit Disorder by Edward M. Hallowell M.D. and John J. Ratey M.D. New York, NY. Ballantine Books. 2005.

How to Mind Map: The Ultimate Thinking Tool that Will Change Your Life by Tony Buzan. London. Thorsons. 2002.

Now, Discover Your Strengths: How to Build Your Strengths and the Strengths of Every Person in Your Organization by Marcus Buckingham and Donald O. Clifton. New York. NY. The Free Press. 2001

The Automatic Millionaire: A Powerful One-Step Plan to Live and Finish Rich by David Bach. Random House of Canada. 2003.

The Four Agreements by Don Miguel Ruiz. Amber Allen Publishing Inc.

RECOMMENDED WEB SITES

ADD Coach Academy....... www.ADDCA.com
ADD Association.............. www.ADD.org
Centre for ADHD Awareness,
Canada .... www.CADDAC.ca
Coach Linda Walker......... www.CoachLindaWalker.com
Focus Action Success Inc... www.FocusActionSuccess.com
The Maximum Productivity Makeover for Creative
Geniuses .... www.MaximumProductivityMakeover.com
Totally ADD...................... www.totallyADD.com

OTHER RECOMMENDED MEDIA

ADD and Loving it, Documentary
on ADHD.......................... www.TotallyADD.com

ABOUT THE AUTHOR

L inda Walker is a serial entrepreneur and the founder of Focus
Action Success Inc. As an ICF Professional Certified Coach,
she works with entrepreneurs, artists, adults with Attention
Deficit Hyperactive Disorder (ADHD) and other creative geniuses destined for greatness. She is the creator of many empowering learning programs including The Maximum Productivity
Makeover for Creative Geniuses.

Linda is a sought-after speaker noted for her passion, energy
and empowering message. Her philosophy focuses on unleash-
ing her audience's creative genius and inspiring them to live their
dreams. She offers one-on-one and group coaching and work-
shops for creative geniuses (in English and French) around the
world.

Her articles on entrepreneurship, productivity, creativity and succeeding as a creative genius have appeared in magazines and newspapers including Success, Home-Based Business, The National Post and The Gazette. She is regularly published in ADHD-related journals and electronic publications. Learn more at her blog at www.coachlindawalker.com/blog.

Linda lives in Montreal, Canada with her artist husband, Duane Gordon, and her youngest daughter Kyrie, both of whom have ADHD.

TO RECEIVE YOUR FREE GIFT RESERVED ESPECIALLY FOR YOU,
AS A READER OF WITH TIME TO SPARE.

WWW.COACHLINDAWALKER.COM/WITHTIMETOSPARE